Functional Backends with Elixir

A Developer Guide to Leverage Pattern Matching and Processes for Efficient Development

Jamie Leslie

Copyright © 2024 Jamie Leslie

All rights reserved. No part of this book may be reproduced, stored in a retrieval system, or transmitted, in any form or by any means, electronic, mechanical, photocopying, recording, or otherwise, without the prior written permission of the author, except in the case of brief quotations embodied in critical reviews and certain other noncommercial uses permitted by copyright law.

Table of Contents

Preface 5
Chapter 1: Introduction to Elixir 6
   1.1 What is Elixir 7
   1.2 Unveiling the Erlang Virtual Machine (BEAM) 8
   1.3 Why Elixir for Backend Development 10
Chapter 2: Functional Programming Fundamentals 11
   2.1 Immutability 12
   2.2 Pure Functions 14
   2.3 Recursion 16
Chapter 3: The Elixir Toolbox 20
   3.1 Syntax and Data Structures 20
   3.2 Functions and Modules 22
   3.3 Introduction to Mix 25
Chapter 4: Pattern Matching Prowess 27
   4.1 Deconstructing Data with Destructuring 27
   4.2 Guard Clauses 30
   4.3 Advanced Pattern Matching 34
Chapter 5: Processes in Action 39
   5.1 Lightweight Processes 39
   5.2 Message Passing 43
   5.3 Building Scalable Applications with Processes 47
Chapter 6: Building Powerful Backends with Elixir 52
   6.1 Phoenix 52
   6.2 Ecto 56
   6.3 Choosing the Right Framework for Your Backend Needs 60
Chapter 7: Elixir - The Elixir of High-Performance APIs 64
   7.1 Designing RESTful APIs with Phoenix 64
   7.2 Handling Requests Efficiently with Concurrency 67
   7.3 Building Secure and Scalable APIs in Elixir 71
Chapter 8: Concurrency in Action 76
   8.1 Handling Asynchronous Requests with Processes 76

    8.2 Real-Time Data Processing... 79
    8.3 Building Distributed Systems with Elixir's Concurrency............ 83
Chapter 9: Testing and Debugging in Elixir..88
    9.1 Writing Effective Tests with ExUnit... 88
    9.2 Debugging Concurrent Systems..92
    9.3 Best Practices for Reliable Backend Applications.......................96
Chapter 10: Building Fault-Tolerant Systems..................................100
    10.1 Open Telecom Platform (OTP)... 100
    10.2 Supervisors.. 103
    10.3 GenServers.. 108
Conclusion...113

Preface

Introduction

Are you tired of wrestling with complex codebases and battling scalability issues? Do you dream of building applications that are not only powerful but also clean, maintainable, and fun to work with? Well, then buckle up, because you're about to embark on an exciting adventure into the world of functional backend development with Elixir!

Background and Motivation

Let's face it, traditional backend development can feel like trying to juggle chainsaws while riding a unicycle. Frameworks come and go, code complexity explodes, and concurrency headaches leave you reaching for the aspirin. But there's a better way!

Elixir, a powerful language built on the rock-solid Erlang VM, offers a breath of fresh air. It combines the elegance of functional programming with the battle-tested concurrency features of Erlang, making it perfect for building robust, scalable backend applications.

Purpose and Scope

This book is your comprehensive guide to unlocking the power of Elixir for backend development. We'll ditch the jargon and focus on practical, hands-on learning. Here's what you can expect:

- Grasp the core concepts of Elixir and functional programming.
- Master pattern matching, Elixir's secret weapon for data manipulation.
- Leverage processes for efficient concurrency and building scalable systems.
- Explore popular frameworks like Phoenix and Ecto for building high-performance APIs and interacting with databases in a functional way.
- Design and implement real-world backend applications using Elixir's magic.

This book is not a dry academic tome. We'll keep things engaging with clear explanations, practical examples, and a touch of humor (because who says coding can't be fun?).

Target Audience

Whether you're a seasoned backend developer looking for a new paradigm, or a curious programmer eager to explore the world of functional programming, this book is for you. No prior knowledge of Elixir is assumed, but a basic understanding of programming concepts will be helpful.

Organization and Structure

The book is structured in a clear, step-by-step manner. We'll start by setting the foundation with the core concepts of Elixir and functional programming. Then, we'll dive deeper into powerful tools like pattern matching and processes. Finally, we'll put everything together by building real-world backend applications with popular frameworks.

Invitation to Read

So, are you ready to write cleaner code, build more scalable applications, and have fun while doing it? Join me on this exciting journey as we unlock the potential of Elixir for backend development! Let's rewrite the rules and build the future of backends, together!

Chapter 1: Introduction to Elixir

This chapter serves as your entry point to the exciting world of Elixir for backend development. We'll begin by exploring what makes Elixir such a compelling choice for building robust and scalable backend applications.

1.1 What is Elixir

The world of backend development is constantly in flux. Established languages and frameworks have served us well, but they can sometimes lead to complex codebases and challenges with scaling applications to meet growing demands. Here's where Elixir enters the scene, offering a fresh perspective with unique strengths.

Elixir is a general-purpose programming language specifically designed for building robust and scalable applications. It accomplishes this by leveraging the power of the Erlang Virtual Machine (BEAM), which we'll discuss in more detail shortly. Elixir itself adheres to a **functional programming paradigm**. This means it emphasizes code that is:

- **Immutable:** Data doesn't change after it's created, leading to more predictable behavior.
- Built with **pure functions:** These functions always produce the same output for the same input, making them easier to test and reason about.
- **Free of side effects:** Pure functions don't modify external states outside their scope, reducing the potential for unexpected behavior.

This functional approach fosters code that's easier to understand, maintain, and test – a significant advantage for complex backend systems.

Beyond Functionals

Another key advantage of Elixir for backend development is its exceptional handling of concurrency. Here's the secret sauce: Elixir leverages the BEAM's robust features to utilize **lightweight processes**, often referred to as actors. These processes operate concurrently, allowing you to tackle multiple tasks simultaneously without the complexities of traditional threading models. This empowers you to build highly responsive and scalable backend applications that can handle a high volume of requests efficiently.

Rock-Solid Reliability

Inheriting from the strengths of Erlang, Elixir is designed with **fault tolerance** in mind. Built-in mechanisms like **supervisors** and **GenServers** help ensure your applications are resilient to errors. In the event of a failure, these features can automatically restart processes or take corrective actions, keeping your backend systems up and running smoothly – a crucial aspect for any reliable backend application.

In summary, Elixir offers a compelling combination of:

- **Functional programming paradigm** for clean, maintainable code.
- **Robust concurrency features** for building highly responsive and scalable applications.
- **Built-in fault tolerance mechanisms** for reliable backend systems.

Whether you're a seasoned backend developer looking for a new approach or a curious programmer exploring functional programming, Elixir offers a powerful set of features that can empower you to build robust, scalable, and maintainable backend applications. In the next sections, we'll delve deeper into the specifics of Elixir and how these features translate into practical benefits for backend development.

1.2 Unveiling the Erlang Virtual Machine (BEAM)

Elixir's power to excel in backend development stems in part from its execution platform, the Erlang Virtual Machine (BEAM). BEAM acts as the foundation for running Elixir code, providing a robust and reliable environment. Here's a breakdown of some key BEAM features that contribute to Elixir's effectiveness:

- **Automatic Memory Management:** BEAM frees developers from the burden of manually allocating and deallocating memory. This is a common source of errors in traditional languages, and BEAM's built-in garbage collection takes care of it automatically.

- **Hot Code Swapping:** Imagine being able to modify the code of a running application without restarting the entire process! BEAM allows for this magic, enabling seamless updates and bug fixes without downtime for your backend systems. This is a significant advantage, especially during deployments.
- **Distributed Processing Powerhouse:** BEAM is specifically designed to handle distributed applications efficiently. This means you can easily distribute processes (which we'll cover later) across multiple machines. This allows you to scale your backend systems horizontally by adding more machines as your application's demands grow.

Let's explore these features in a bit more detail:

- **Garbage Collection Demystified:** In traditional programming, developers need to explicitly manage memory allocation and deallocation. This can be error-prone, as forgetting to free unused memory can lead to memory leaks, and freeing memory too early can cause crashes. BEAM handles this automatically, monitoring memory usage and reclaiming unused memory when necessary. This frees developers to focus on core application logic without worrying about memory management headaches.

- **Hot Code Swapping in Action:** Imagine you've identified and fixed a bug in your backend application. Traditionally, you'd need to stop the entire application, deploy the fix, and then restart everything. BEAM's hot code swapping allows you to make the code change directly on a running system. BEAM detects the update and seamlessly integrates it into the running application, all without any downtime. This significantly streamlines the development and deployment process.

- **Scaling Up with Distributed Processing:** As your backend application gains traction, the number of users and requests it needs to handle will increase. Traditional systems might struggle under this growing load. BEAM's distributed processing capabilities allow you to distribute the workload across multiple machines. This means you can add more machines to your backend infrastructure as needed, effectively scaling your application horizontally to handle increased demands.

By providing these features, BEAM creates a robust and reliable foundation for running Elixir code. Automatic memory management safeguards against errors, hot code swapping streamlines development, and distributed processing empowers you to build highly scalable backend systems. In the next section, we'll see how these BEAM features and Elixir's functional programming style work together to make Elixir shine in backend development.

1.3 Why Elixir for Backend Development

We've explored the strengths of Elixir's programming style and the underlying Erlang Virtual Machine (BEAM). Now, let's see how these elements combine to make Elixir a perfect fit for building powerful backend applications.

Built for Scalability

- **Handling High Traffic with Ease:** Backend applications often deal with a high volume of user requests. Elixir's concurrency features, enabled by BEAM's lightweight processes, come to the rescue. These processes act like mini-programs that can run simultaneously, allowing your application to handle multiple requests at once. This translates to a highly responsive and scalable backend system that can efficiently manage heavy traffic.
- **Always Up and Running:** Failures are inevitable in any system, but for backend applications, downtime can be costly. Elixir inherits fault tolerance features from BEAM. Supervisors can monitor processes, and if a process crashes, the supervisor can automatically restart it. Additionally, GenServers provide a structured way to build stateful and reliable services that can recover from errors gracefully. This combination keeps your backend application up and running smoothly, even when faced with unexpected issues.

Maintainability Matters

- **Clean and Concise with Functional Programming:** Elixir's functional programming paradigm emphasizes immutability, pure functions, and avoiding side effects. This leads to code that is easier to understand, test, and modify in the long run. Imagine a codebase that is clear, predictable, and less prone to errors – that's the beauty of functional programming for backend development!

- **Focus on Core Functionality:** Backend development often involves complex logic. Elixir's features like hot code swapping help streamline the process. Imagine being able to make code changes to a running application without restarting the entire system. This allows developers to focus on core functionalities and iterate quickly, leading to faster development cycles and more efficient backend development.

A Thriving Ecosystem for Success

- **Powerful Libraries and Frameworks:** Elixir benefits from a growing and active community that has developed a rich set of libraries and frameworks specifically designed for backend development. Popular options like Phoenix and Ecto provide pre-built tools for building robust APIs and interacting with databases efficiently. This saves developers time and effort by leveraging pre-existing solutions for common backend tasks.

In essence, Elixir shines in backend development because it offers a unique blend of:

- **Scalability:** Efficient concurrency features to handle high traffic.
- **Fault Tolerance:** Built-in mechanisms to ensure reliable application uptime.
- **Maintainability:** Functional programming for clean and manageable code.
- **Developer Productivity:** Tools and libraries to streamline development.

Whether you're a seasoned backend developer looking for a fresh approach or a curious programmer exploring functional programming, Elixir offers a compelling set of features that can empower you to build modern, robust, and maintainable backend applications.

Chapter 2: Functional Programming Fundamentals

In this chapter, we'll delve into the heart of Elixir – its functional programming soul. Here, we'll explore the key concepts that make Elixir code clean, predictable, and a joy to work with, especially for building robust backend applications.

Imagine a world where your code is like a delicious, perfectly layered cake. Each layer is independent, well-defined, and contributes to the overall sweetness (and functionality) of the final product. That's the beauty of immutability, the first pillar of functional programming we'll explore.

2.1 Immutability

In the realm of backend development, code stability is king. Imagine a complex backend application handling thousands of user requests – the last thing you want is unexpected behavior due to data changes. This is where immutability, a core principle of functional programming, enters the scene.

Immutability Explained:

Simply put, immutability means that data cannot be modified after it's created. Think of it like a historical document – once written, its content remains fixed. In Elixir, when you assign a value to a variable, that variable holds a reference to a copy of the data, not the original data itself. This creates a clear distinction:

- **Variable:** A symbolic name referencing a piece of data.
- **Data:** The actual value stored in memory.

Here's an example to illustrate:

Elixir

```
name = "Elixir"  # Variable 'name' references a copy of the string "Elixir"
# Trying to modify the data through the variable won't work!
```

```
name = name ++ " is awesome"  # This creates a new string, not
modifying the original "Elixir"
IO.puts name  # This will still print "Elixir"
```

In this example, the variable name initially references the string "Elixir." Assigning a new string using the ++ operator doesn't modify the original data referenced by name. Instead, a new string "Elixir is awesome" is created, and name is reassigned to reference this new string.

Benefits of Immutability for Backend Development:

- **Enhanced Debugging:** Since data remains unchanged, tracing the origin of errors becomes easier. You can pinpoint exactly where a value was created and see its history.
- **Improved Thread Safety:** In multi-threaded backend systems (which we'll explore later!), immutability prevents race conditions. These occur when multiple threads try to modify the same data simultaneously, leading to unpredictable results. With immutability, each thread works with a copy of the data, avoiding conflicts.
- **Clearer and More Maintainable Code:** Immutability promotes code that's easier to reason about. You know precisely what a variable represents at any given point, making your backend code more understandable and easier to maintain for yourself and your team.

Immutability in Practice

Elixir provides several ways to work with immutable data:

- **Creating New Values:** As we saw earlier, assignment (= operator) creates a copy of the data.
- **Functions and Immutability:** Ideally, functions should not modify existing data but rather return new data structures reflecting the desired changes.

Here's an example demonstrating this concept:

Elixir

```
def update_name(name, new_name) do
  # Return a new string with the updated name
```

```
    "#{name} the Great"
end
updated_name = update_name("Elixir", "Phoenix")
IO.puts updated_name  # This will print "Elixir the Great" (without
modifying the original "Elixir")
```
In this example, the update_name function doesn't modify the original name variable. Instead, it returns a new string with the updated value.

Embrace Immutability

Immutability might seem like a departure from traditional programming, but its benefits for building reliable and maintainable backend applications are undeniable. As you delve deeper into Elixir, you'll discover that immutability becomes second nature, leading to cleaner, more predictable, and robust backend code.

2.2 Pure Functions

Imagine a world where your backend functions are like trusty vending machines. You feed them the same input (coins), and they consistently dispense the same output (candy bar). This unwavering predictability is the essence of pure functions, a cornerstone of functional programming in Elixir. Let's explore why pure functions are rock stars for building robust backend applications.

A pure function is a special type of function that adheres to three key principles:

- **Input-Output Harmony:** They always produce the same output for a given set of inputs. This predictability makes them incredibly reliable and easier to test in your backend code.
- **No Side Effects:** Pure functions don't modify any external state (like global variables) outside their scope. This keeps your code clean and avoids unexpected behavior that can plague complex backend applications.
- **Reusable Rocket Fuel:** Since pure functions only rely on their inputs, you can reuse them throughout your backend application without worrying about unintended consequences.

Benefits of Pure Functions for Backend Development

- **Enhanced Testability:** With predictable behavior, testing pure functions becomes a breeze. You know exactly what output to expect for a given input, making unit testing a reliable way to ensure your backend functions work as intended.
- **Simplified Debugging:** Since pure functions don't have side effects, pinpointing the source of errors becomes easier. You can isolate the function that's causing the issue and focus your debugging efforts there.
- **Improved Code Maintainability:** Pure functions are generally easier to understand and reason about. Their predictable behavior and lack of side effects make your backend code cleaner and more maintainable in the long run.

Pure Functions in Action:

Let's look at some code examples to illustrate pure functions in Elixir:

Elixir

```elixir
def add(x, y) do
  x + y
end
# Calling the function with different inputs
result1 = add(2, 3)  # result1 will be 5
result2 = add(5, 8)  # result2 will be 13
IO.puts result1  # This will print 5
IO.puts result2  # This will print 13
```

This add function perfectly demonstrates a pure function. It takes two numbers as input (x and y), performs the addition operation, and returns the result. No matter how many times you call it with the same inputs, it will always return the sum. Additionally, it doesn't modify any external state, making it a reliable building block for your backend application.

Beyond Simple Math:

Pure functions can be used for more complex tasks as well. Here's an example that calculates the length of a list:

Elixir

```elixir
def list_length(list) do
  # Base case: Empty list has a length of 0
  if list == [], do: 0
  # Recursive call: Remove the head and call list_length on the tail
  head = List.head(list)
  tail = List.tl(list)
  1 + list_length(tail)
end
my_list = [1, 2, 3, 4]
list_length(my_list)  # This will return 4
```

This list_length function showcases a recursive pure function. It checks for the base case (empty list) and then recursively calls itself on the tail of the list until it reaches the end. In each iteration, it adds 1 to the result of the recursive call, effectively calculating the total length. Although this example uses recursion, it remains a pure function as it follows the core principles: predictable output for a given input and no side effects.

By leveraging pure functions in your backend development, you gain a significant advantage. Their predictable nature leads to cleaner, more testable, and more maintainable code. As you explore Elixir further, you'll discover that pure functions become instrumental in building robust and reliable backend applications.

2.3 Recursion

Alright, folks, buckle up for a concept that might sound mind-bending at first, but trust me, it's a powerful tool in your Elixir toolbox for building backend applications! We're venturing into the world of recursion – a technique where a function calls itself. Hold on, don't get discouraged by the seemingly circular logic. Let's break it down and see how recursion can become your secret weapon for tackling repetitive tasks with elegance.

Imagine you have a curious child who keeps asking "why?" Recursion works in a similar way. A recursive function breaks down a problem into smaller, similar subproblems. Then, here's the twist – it calls itself to solve those subproblems! Each recursive call works on a smaller piece of the puzzle until it reaches a base case (a simple condition that doesn't require further recursion) and then starts working its way back up, combining the solutions from each call to solve the original problem entirely.

Think of it like peeling an onion. You keep removing layers (solving subproblems) until you reach the core (the final solution). While it might seem counterintuitive at first, recursion can be incredibly effective for certain tasks, especially when dealing with data structures like lists.

Why Use Recursion for Backend Development?

Here's the beauty of recursion:
- **Elegant Solutions for Repetitive Tasks:** Many backend development tasks involve working with data structures like lists. Recursion allows you to write concise and readable code that iterates through these structures in a natural, step-by-step manner.
- **Improved Code Readability:** For problems that can be solved recursively, the code itself can often become more readable and easier to understand compared to traditional iterative approaches using loops. Imagine explaining your code to a teammate – recursion can sometimes make that explanation much clearer.
- **Powerful with Lists:** Recursion shines when working with lists. By calling itself on smaller and smaller sub-lists, it can elegantly solve problems like calculating sums, finding elements, or reversing the order of elements.

Let's See Recursion in Action!

Alright, enough talk, let's see some code! Here's an example of a recursive function that calculates the factorial of a number (factorial of a number is all the positive integers multiplied together from that number down to 1).

Elixir

```elixir
def factorial(number) do
  # Base case: Factorial of 0 is 1
  if number == 0, do: 1
  # Recursive call: number * factorial(number - 1)
  number * factorial(number - 1)
end
```

factorial(5) # This will return 120 (5 * 4 * 3 * 2 * 1)

In this example, the factorial function checks if the number is 0. If so, that's the base case, and the function returns 1 (factorial of 0). Otherwise, it performs a recursive call. It multiplies the current number by the factorial of the previous number (achieved by another recursive call). This process continues until it reaches the base case (factorial of 0), and then the results are multiplied together as each recursive call returns.

Here are more additional examples of recursion in Elixir to illustrate its versatility for backend development tasks:

1. **Reversing a List:**

This example demonstrates how recursion can be used to reverse the order of elements in a list.

Elixir

```
def reverse_list(list) do
  # Base case: Empty list or single element is already reversed
  if list == [] || List.length(list) == 1, do: list
  # Recursive call: Get the head and tail of the list
  head = List.head(list)
  tail = List.tl(list)
  # Reverse the tail and prepend the head to the reversed tail
  reverse_list(tail) ++ [head]
end
my_list = [1, 2, 3, 4]
reverse_list(my_list)  # This will return [4, 3, 2, 1]
```

2. **Calculating the Sum of a List:**

This example showcases recursion for summing up the elements in a list.

Elixir

```
def sum_list(list) do
  # Base case: Empty list has a sum of 0
  if list == [], do: 0
  # Recursive call: Get the head and tail of the list
  head = List.head(list)
  tail = List.tl(list)
```

```elixir
  # Add the head to the sum of the tail (recursive call)
  head + sum_list(tail)
end
my_list = [5, 8, 2]

sum_list(my_list)  # This will return 15 (5 + 8 + 2)
```

3. **Finding an Element in a List:**

   This example uses recursion to search for a specific element within a list.

```elixir
Elixir
def find_element(list, element) do
  # Base case: Empty list or element not found
  if list == [], do: nil
  # Recursive call: Check if the head matches the element
  head = List.head(list)
  tail = List.tl(list)
  if head == element do
    element  # Element found, return it
  else
    find_element(tail, element)  # Recursive call on the tail
  end
end
my_list = ["apple", "banana", "orange"]
find_element(my_list, "banana")  # This will return "banana"
```

These examples showcase the diverse applications of recursion in backend development.

Recursion might take some practice to get comfortable with, but don't be discouraged! As you start using it for repetitive tasks in your backend applications, you'll discover its elegance and power. Remember, there are also situations where iterative solutions using loops might be more efficient. The key is to understand both approaches and choose the one that best suits your specific problem.

So, the next time you encounter a repetitive task in your backend development, consider the power of recursion! It might just become your go-to tool for crafting clean, readable, and elegant solutions.

Chapter 3: The Elixir Toolbox

Now that we've explored the core principles of functional programming, it's time to delve into the practical side of things. This chapter equips you with the essential tools in the Elixir toolbox, specifically designed to build robust and maintainable backend applications.

3.1 Syntax and Data Structures

Welcome to the foundation of your Elixir adventure! Just like any construction project, building robust backend applications requires a solid understanding of the basic building blocks. In Elixir, these come in the form of syntax and data structures.

Elixir Syntax

Imagine a language that feels almost like writing instructions in plain English. That's the beauty of Elixir's syntax! It relies on keywords, operators, and expressions to define the functionality of your backend application. Here's a breakdown of the key elements:

- **Keywords:** These are reserved words that have a specific meaning within the Elixir language. For example, def is used to define functions, and if is used for conditional statements.
- **Operators:** Operators perform operations on data. You'll encounter arithmetic operators (+, -, *, /), comparison operators (==, !=, <, >), and many more, similar to other programming languages.
- **Expressions:** Expressions combine variables, operators, and function calls to create a value or perform an action. For instance, 2 + 3 is an expression that evaluates to 5.

Here's a simple example to illustrate Elixir syntax:

Elixir
```
name = "Elixir"  # Assigning a string value to a variable
age = 10  # Assigning an integer value to a variable
if age >= 18 do
   IO.puts "Welcome, #{name}! You can now access adult features."  # Conditional statement with string interpolation
end
```

In this example, we define variables (name and age), use an if statement for conditional logic, and leverage string interpolation (#{name}) to embed a variable within a string.

Data Structures

Just like a toolbox holds various tools for different tasks, your backend application will rely on various data structures to store and organize information. Here are some of the most commonly used data structures in Elixir:

- **Lists:** Ordered collections of items, similar to arrays in other languages. You can store elements of different data types within a list. Lists are great for representing sequences of data.

    Elixir

    my_list = [1, "apple", true] # List containing an integer, a string, and a boolean

- **Maps:** Collections of key-value pairs, similar to dictionaries in other languages. Maps allow you to associate unique keys with specific values, making them ideal for storing structured data.

    Elixir

    user_data = %{name: "John", age: 30, email: "john@example.com"} # Map with key-value pairs for user information

- **Tuples:** Fixed-length ordered sequences of elements. Tuples are immutable (unchangeable), meaning their elements cannot be modified once created. They are useful for representing data structures where order matters.

    Elixir

    coordinates = {25, 37} # Tuple representing a location with x and y coordinates

- **Atoms:** Atoms are like unique symbols that represent themselves. They are often used for constants or categories within your application.

  Elixir

  :ok # An atom representing success

  :error # An atom representing an error

  Choosing the Right Tool for the Job

  As you become familiar with these data structures, you'll discover their strengths and weaknesses. Here are some general guidelines:
- **Lists:** Use lists when you need an ordered collection of items that may vary in type.
- **Maps:** Use maps when you need to store structured data with key-value pairs for easy access.
- **Tuples:** Use tuples when you need a fixed-length ordered sequence where the order is significant.
- **Atoms:** Use atoms for constants or categories that represent specific concepts within your application.

Embrace the Power of Building Blocks

By mastering Elixir syntax and data structures, you'll lay a solid foundation for building powerful backend applications. The clear and expressive syntax makes your code readable, while the versatile data structures provide the tools to organize and manage your application's data effectively. As we move forward in this chapter, we'll delve deeper into each data structure and explore how to use them to their full potential in your backend development journey.

3.2 Functions and Modules

Imagine a sprawling backend application – a labyrinth of code that's difficult to navigate and maintain. Elixir equips you with two powerful tools to prevent this chaos: functions and modules. Let's explore how they can keep your code organized and efficient.

Functions

Think of functions as the workhorses of your Elixir code. They are self-contained blocks of code that perform specific tasks and return outputs. Here's a breakdown of the key aspects of functions:

- **Definition:** You define functions using the def keyword, followed by the function name, parameters (inputs), and the function body (the code that executes the task).
- **Parameters:** These are like placeholders that allow you to pass data into the function when you call it. Imagine parameters as ingredients you pass to a recipe (the function).
- **Return Values:** Functions can optionally return a value using the return keyword. This value becomes the output of the function, similar to how a recipe yields a finished dish.

Here's an example of a simple function that greets a user:

Elixir

```elixir
def greet(name) do
  IO.puts "Hello, #{name}!"
end
greet("Elixir Developer")  # This will print "Hello, Elixir Developer!"
```

In this example, the greet function takes a parameter name and uses string interpolation to personalize the greeting. When you call the function with "Elixir Developer" as an argument, it becomes the value assigned to the name parameter within the function, resulting in the customized greeting.

Benefits of Functions:

- **Reusability:** Functions promote code reusability. You can define a function once and call it from different parts of your code whenever you need that specific functionality. This reduces code duplication and keeps your application organized.
- **Modularity:** Functions break down complex tasks into smaller, manageable steps. This makes your code easier to understand, maintain, and test.

- **Readability:** Well-named functions with clear comments enhance the readability of your code. Imagine explaining your code to a teammate – functions act as building blocks that make that explanation much clearer.

Modules

As your backend application grows, the number of functions will inevitably increase. Here's where modules come into play:
- **Definition:** Modules are namespaces that group related functions and data together. Think of them as folders in your codebase, keeping things organized and categorized.
- **Scoping:** Modules provide a way to control the visibility of functions and data. Functions defined within a module are private by default, accessible only from within that module. This helps prevent naming conflicts and promotes better code organization.

Here's an example of a module for handling user-related functions:

Elixir

```elixir
defmodule User do
  def create(name, email) do
    # Code to create a new user with the given name and email
  end
  def get(user_id) do
    # Code to retrieve user information based on the ID
  end
end
```

In this example, the User module encapsulates two functions: create for creating new users and get for retrieving user information. These functions are private by default, accessible only within the User module itself.

Benefits of Modules:

- **Organization:** Modules help organize your codebase by grouping related functions and data. This makes it easier to find and manage code as your application grows in complexity.
- **Namespace Management:** Modules prevent naming conflicts by providing a way to scope function and data names. Imagine having two

functions named greet in different parts of your code – modules help avoid confusion.

- **Readability:** Well-organized modules with clear names enhance the readability and maintainability of your backend application.

Working Together: Functions and Modules in Harmony

Functions and modules work hand-in-hand to create a well-structured and maintainable backend application. Functions act as reusable building blocks, while modules organize these functions and data into logical units. This combination promotes code reusability, readability, and efficient development.

As you delve deeper into Elixir development, you'll discover the power of functions and modules in crafting robust and scalable backend applications. Remember, using these tools effectively is key to building clean and maintainable code that can evolve with your project's needs.

3.3 Introduction to Mix

Imagine building a house – you wouldn't start hammering nails without a blueprint and the right tools. Similarly, in Elixir development, Mix acts as your essential toolbox for building, testing, and managing your backend projects. Let's explore what Mix brings to the table:

Mix

Mix is a build tool that comes bundled with Elixir. It streamlines various tasks throughout your development workflow, saving you time and effort. Here's a breakdown of its key functionalities:
- **Project Creation:** Tired of setting up project directories and configurations manually? Mix offers a quick and easy way to create new Elixir projects with the necessary structure and dependencies already in place. Simply run a Mix command, and you're ready to start coding!
- **Compilation:** Elixir code needs to be compiled into bytecode before it can be executed by the Erlang virtual machine (BEAM). Mix handles this compilation process seamlessly. Just run a Mix command, and your code will be transformed into a format the machine understands.
- **Testing:** Robust backend applications rely on thorough testing. Mix integrates with various testing frameworks, allowing you to write unit tests and ensure your code functions as expected. You can run tests

directly from the command line using Mix, catching any errors early in the development process.
- **Dependency Management:** Most backend applications rely on external libraries and tools. Mix simplifies dependency management by allowing you to specify dependencies in your project configuration. Mix then takes care of downloading and managing these dependencies for you.
- **Running the Application:** Once your code is compiled and tested, you're ready to launch your backend application! Mix provides commands to start your application, making it easy to deploy and run your code in production environments.

Here's an example of how you might use Mix to create a new Elixir project and run it:

Bash

```
mix new my_backend_app  # Creates a new project named "my_backend_app"
cd my_backend_app  # Navigate into the project directory
mix compile  # Compiles your Elixir code
mix test  # Runs any unit tests you've written
mix run  # Starts your backend application
```

Beyond the Basics
While these are the core functionalities, Mix offers additional features for advanced backend development:
- **Hot Code Reloading:** Imagine making a code change and seeing it reflected in your running application instantly. Mix supports hot code reloading, allowing you to make changes and see the results without restarting your application, streamlining the development process.

- **Tasks:** Mix allows you to define custom tasks within your project. This lets you automate repetitive tasks specific to your application's needs.

Embrace Efficiency with Mix

By leveraging Mix effectively, you can significantly improve your backend development workflow. It saves you time on manual tasks, helps manage dependencies, and ensures your code is well-tested and ready for production. As you progress in your Elixir journey, Mix will become your go-to tool for building and maintaining robust backend applications.

Chapter 4: Pattern Matching Prowess

We've explored the building blocks and tools in our Elixir toolbox. Now, it's time to refine your skills with a powerful technique called pattern matching. Buckle up, because this chapter will transform you from a data-wrangling novice to a pattern-matching ninja!

4.1 Deconstructing Data with Destructuring

Imagine receiving a beautifully wrapped gift – a box filled with mystery! Destructuring in Elixir allows you to approach data structures in a similar way, unwrapping them with elegance and precision. In this section, we'll explore how destructuring helps you extract specific values from lists, maps, and tuples in a clear and concise manner.

Destructuring

Destructuring is a powerful technique in Elixir that lets you extract specific values from data structures like lists, maps, and tuples. It's like carefully peeling back the layers of your gift to reveal the treasures within, but with code! Here's a breakdown of the key concepts:

- **Data Structures:** Remember, data structures are like containers that hold information in a specific format. Lists hold ordered sequences of items, maps store key-value pairs, and tuples are fixed-length ordered sequences.
- **Extracting Values:** Destructuring allows you to target specific values within these data structures and assign them to variables with meaningful names. This makes your code more readable and avoids the need for cumbersome techniques like indexing or using map keys repeatedly.

Destructuring Lists: Unpacking Orderly Elements

Let's see how destructuring works with lists:

Elixir

```
my_list = ["Elixir", 10, true]
# Traditional Method (less clear)
first_element = my_list[1]  # Accessing the second element (index starts from 0)
```

```
second_element = my_list[2]
IO.puts first_element  # This will print "Elixir"
IO.puts second_element  # This will print 10
```

In this traditional approach, we use indexing to access specific elements within the list. While it works, it can become cumbersome for longer lists.

Elixir

```
# Destructuring Method (more concise and readable)
[name, age, is_active] = my_list
IO.puts name  # This will print "Elixir"
IO.puts age  # This will print 10
IO.puts is_active  # This will print true
```

Here, we leverage destructuring! The pattern on the left-hand side ([name, age, is_active]) defines the expected structure of the list (three elements). The assignment on the right-hand side extracts those elements and assigns them to variables with descriptive names, making the code much more readable.

Destructuring Maps: Unpacking Key-Value Pairs

Maps, which store key-value pairs, can also be destructured to extract specific values:

Elixir

```
user_data = %{name: "John", email: "john@example.com"}
# Traditional Method (less clear)
user_name = user_data[:name]
user_email = user_data[:email]
IO.puts user_name  # This will print "John"
IO.puts user_email  # This will print "john@example.com"
```

This traditional method relies on accessing values using map keys. While functional, it can become repetitive and less readable for maps with many key-value pairs.

Elixir

```
# Destructuring Method (more concise and readable)
%{name: user_name, email: user_email} = user_data
IO.puts user_name  # This will print "John"
```

IO.puts user_email # This will print "john@example.com"

Destructuring allows us to directly specify the keys (name and email) we're interested in and assign the corresponding values to variables with more descriptive names (user_name and user_email). This enhances code readability and reduces the need to repeat map keys.

Benefits of Destructuring

- **Readability:** Destructuring improves code readability by making it clear how you're extracting values from data structures. Imagine explaining your code to a teammate – destructuring makes that explanation much clearer.
- **Conciseness:** Destructuring eliminates the need for cumbersome indexing or accessing values with map keys. It allows you to write cleaner and more compact code.
- **Error Handling:** Destructuring can implicitly handle situations where the data structure doesn't match the expected pattern. This helps you catch potential errors early on.

By mastering destructuring, you'll be able to efficiently extract and work with specific values within your Elixir data structures, keeping your code clean, concise, and easy to understand. In the next section, we'll explore how to add conditional checks within your destructuring patterns using guard clauses.

Here are some additional examples and code snippets to further illustrate destructuring in Elixir:

Destructuring Lists with Different Lengths:

Elixir

```
# List with two elements
[name, age] = ["Alice", 25]
IO.puts name  # This will print "Alice"
IO.puts age  # This will print 25
# List with one element (remaining elements assigned to nil)
[name, age] = ["Bob"]
IO.puts name  # This will print "Bob"
IO.puts age  # This will print nil
```

```elixir
# List with more elements than expected (remaining elements
discarded)
[name, age, _] = ["Charlie", 30, "New York"]
IO.puts name  # This will print "Charlie"
IO.puts age   # This will print 30
```

Destructuring Tuples:

Tuples, which are fixed-length ordered sequences, can also be destructured:

Elixir

```elixir
coordinates = {23, 42}
{x, y} = coordinates
IO.puts x  # This will print 23

IO.puts y  # This will print 42
```

Destructuring Maps with Different Keys:

Elixir

```elixir
user_info = %{name: "David", age: 40, city: "London"}
# Destructuring with specific keys
%{name: user_name, age: user_age} = user_info
IO.puts user_name  # This will print "David"
IO.puts user_age   # This will print 40
# Destructuring with missing keys (defaults to nil)
%{name: user_name, email: user_email} = user_info
IO.puts user_email  # This will print nil (email key not present)
```

These examples showcase how destructuring can handle lists and tuples of varying lengths, as well as maps with missing keys. Remember, destructuring offers a concise and readable way to extract specific values from your Elixir data structures.

4.2 Guard Clauses

Imagine you're sorting mail – you need a way to check the destination address before delivering it. Similarly, in Elixir's pattern matching, guard clauses act like intelligent mail sorters, allowing you to add conditional checks within your patterns for more precise control.

While destructuring helps extract values, guard clauses let you specify additional conditions that must be met for the pattern match to succeed. Think of them as filters within your pattern matching logic, ensuring only the "correct data" passes through for further processing.

Syntax and Structure:

- **Placement:** Guard clauses are placed within parentheses after the pattern itself.
- **Conditional Expressions:** They use conditional expressions like if statements to perform checks on the extracted values.

Here's an example illustrating a guard clause:

Elixir

[name, age] when age >= 18 = ["Elixir", 25] do
    IO.puts "Welcome, #{name}! You can access adult features."

end

Explanation:

1. **Pattern Matching:** The pattern [name, age] still destructures the list into name and age variables.

2. **Guard Clause:** The when age >= 18 part acts as the filter. Only if the age is greater than or equal to 18 will the code within the do block execute.

Benefits of Guard Clauses:

- **Improved Readability:** Guard clauses keep your code concise and readable by integrating conditional checks within the pattern matching itself. Imagine explaining your code to a teammate – guard clauses make conditional logic within patterns much clearer.
- **Early Exits:** If a condition fails in a guard clause, the pattern match doesn't proceed. This allows for early exits, preventing unnecessary code execution and improving performance.

- **Error Handling:** Guard clauses can be used to handle unexpected data or errors within the pattern matching logic. For instance, you could check if a key exists in a map before trying to access its value.
  Additional Examples of Guard Clauses:

- **Checking for Specific Values:**

  Elixir

  ```
  color = "red" when color == "red" or color == "blue" do
    IO.puts "The color is either red or blue."
  End
  ```

- **Matching Against a Range:**

  Elixir

  ```
  grade = 85 when grade >= 70 and grade <= 100 do
    IO.puts "You got a B!"
  end
  ```

- **Checking for Data Types:**

  Elixir

  ```
  user_input = "25" when is_integer(user_input) do
    # Convert the string to an integer before processing
    user_age = String.to_integer(user_input)
    IO.puts "Your age is #{user_age}."
  end
  ```

Here are some additional examples and code snippets to further illustrate guard clauses in Elixir:

Nesting Guard Clauses:

You can nest multiple guard clauses within a pattern for more complex conditional checks:

Elixir
```
order = %{items: ["book", "pencil"], total: 20}
when order.total >= 15 and order.items[:length] > 1 do
```

IO.puts "You qualify for free shipping!"
end

In this example, the guard clause checks two conditions:
1. The order total must be greater than or equal to 15.
2. The number of items in the order (accessed using order.items[:length]) must be greater than 1.

Using Guard Clauses for Default Values:

Guard clauses can be used to assign default values if a condition fails:

Elixir
user_data = %{name: "Alice"}
name = user_data.name || "Anonymous"
IO.puts name # This will print "Alice"
user_data = %{} # Empty map
name = user_data.name || "Anonymous"
IO.puts name # This will print "Anonymous" (default value)

Here, the guard clause checks if the name key exists in the map. If it does, the value is assigned to the name variable. If not, the default value "Anonymous" is used.

Matching Against Multiple Patterns:

Guard clauses can be used with multiple patterns to define different processing logic for each case:
Elixir
status = :ok
message = "Operation successful!"
status = :error when status == :error and is_binary(message) do
  IO.puts "Error: #{message}"
end
status = :warning when status == :warning do
  IO.puts "Warning encountered."
end

IO.puts "Status: #{status}" # This will print "Status: ok"

In this example, the first pattern matches the :ok status with any message. The second pattern matches the :error status with a binary message (string), printing the error message. The third pattern handles the :warning status.

These examples demonstrate the flexibility of guard clauses in pattern matching. They allow you to create sophisticated conditional logic within your patterns, enhancing the control and efficiency of your Elixir code.

These examples showcase the versatility of guard clauses. They allow you to perform various checks on the extracted values, ensuring your pattern matching logic is precise and efficient.

Guard clauses empower you to add conditional checks within your pattern matching, making your Elixir code more robust and readable. By combining destructuring and guard clauses, you can effectively extract and analyze data while ensuring only the relevant information proceeds for further processing. In the next section, we'll explore advanced pattern matching techniques that unlock even more powerful ways to work with complex data structures in Elixir.

4.3 Advanced Pattern Matching

Elixir's pattern matching goes beyond the basics of destructuring and guard clauses. It offers powerful techniques for analyzing and working with complex data structures. In this section, we'll explore some of these advanced features:

1. Matching Against Any Value

Imagine you're working with a list of user preferences, but some users might not have specific preferences set yet. The wildcard operator (_) allows you to match against any value in a specific position within a pattern.

Here's an example:

Elixir

```
user_prefs = ["music", "movies", _] # User might not have a third preference
```

```elixir
# Traditional Method (less flexible)
if length(user_prefs) >= 3 do
  third_pref = user_prefs[3]
  IO.puts "Third preference: #{third_pref}"
end
# Using Wildcard Operator (more concise)
[pref1, pref2, _] = user_prefs
IO.puts "Third preference (if any): #{elem(user_prefs, 3)}"  # Access using elem if needed
```

In this example:

- The traditional method uses an if statement to check the list length and access the third element if it exists.

- The pattern matching with the wildcard operator (_) is more concise. It simply discards the third element without needing an if statement. You can still access the third element using elem(user_prefs, 3) if needed.

2. Pattern Matching with Nested Data Structures

Elixir allows you to match against nested data structures like lists within lists or maps within maps. This is particularly useful for processing complex data hierarchies:

Elixir

```elixir
user_data = %{
  name: "Bob",
  address: %{
    street: "123 Main St",
    city: "Anytown"
  }
}

# Traditional Method (less readable)
address = user_data.address
city = address.city if address
# Using Nested Pattern Matching (more readable)
%{name: name, address: %{city: city}} = user_data
IO.puts "City: #{city}"
```

Here, the nested pattern matching directly extracts the city from the nested address map, improving code readability.

3. Recursive Pattern Matching

For deeply nested data structures, recursive pattern matching allows you to define patterns that can match against structures at any depth. Imagine peeling an onion layer by layer – recursive patterns work similarly.

Here's a simplified example (assuming a nested list structure):

Elixir

```
defmodule ListParser do
  def parse(list) do
    case list do
      [head | tail] -> IO.puts "Head: #{head}, Tail: #{tail}"
      [] -> IO.puts "Empty list"
      _ -> IO.puts "Unexpected data type"  # Handle unexpected data
    end
    parse(tail)  # Recursive call to process the tail (if not empty)
  end
end
```

ListParser.parse([1, [2, 3], 4])
This example defines a recursive function parse that uses pattern matching:
- It matches a list with a head element (head) and a tail (tail).
- It matches an empty list ([]).
- It has a catch-all pattern (_) to handle unexpected data types.

The function then recursively calls itself on the tail of the list, continuing the pattern matching process until the list is empty.

Here are some additional examples and code snippets to further illustrate advanced pattern matching techniques in Elixir

1. Matching Against Tuples with Specific Elements:

While wildcards can match any value, you can also use specific elements within tuples:

```elixir
response = {:ok, 200, "Success message"}

# Matching the entire tuple
case response do
  {:ok, code, message} when code == 200 ->
    IO.puts "Request successful! Message: #{message}"
end

# Matching specific elements (ignoring others with _)
case response do
  {:ok, _, _} ->
    IO.puts "Request successful (ignoring code and message)"
end
```

2. Pattern Matching with Keyword Lists:

Keyword lists, used for passing optional arguments to functions, can also be matched against patterns:

```elixir
def greet(name \\ "World") do
  IO.puts "Hello, #{name}!"
end
greet()  # Matches default name ("World")

greet(name: "Alice")  # Matches the name key-value pair
```

3. Recursive Pattern Matching for Complex Lists:

Here's a more detailed example of recursive pattern matching for complex lists:

```elixir
defmodule ListProcessor do
  def process(list) do
    case list do
      [head | [tail1, tail2]] ->
        IO.puts "Head: #{head}, Sublists: #{tail1}, #{tail2}"
        process(tail1)
```

```
      process(tail2)
    [head | tail] ->
      IO.puts "Head: #{head}, Tail: #{tail}"
      process(tail)
    [] ->
      IO.puts "Empty list"
  end
 end
end
```

ListProcessor.process([1, [2, 3], 4, [5, 6]])
This example demonstrates recursive calls to process both sublists within the main list, showcasing how pattern matching can handle nested data structures effectively.

These examples provide a glimpse into the versatility of advanced pattern matching in Elixir. By combining these techniques, you can create powerful and flexible solutions for working with complex data in your Elixir applications.

Advanced Techniques for Experienced Developers

Elixir offers even more advanced pattern matching features like:
- **Matching Against Functions:** You can match against functions themselves, allowing for dynamic pattern definitions.
- **Matching Against Pines:** Pines (^) allow you to temporarily bind a value during pattern matching without permanent assignment.

In Conclusion:
Advanced pattern matching techniques in Elixir unlock powerful ways to analyze and manipulate complex data structures. By understanding wildcards, nested patterns, and recursion, you can write concise, readable, and efficient code for handling even the most intricate data in your backend applications. Remember, mastering these techniques will make you a true Elixir pattern matching ninja!

Chapter 5: Processes in Action

We've explored the building blocks and pattern matching techniques that make Elixir a fantastic language. Now, it's time to delve into the heart of what makes Elixir truly unique: its power in handling concurrency. Buckle up, because this chapter will transform you from a single-threaded warrior to a master of concurrent processes!

5.1 Lightweight Processes

Imagine a bustling coffee shop. Baristas juggle multiple tasks – brewing coffee, steaming milk, taking orders – all at the same time. This ability to handle many tasks concurrently is essential for a smooth-running shop. Similarly, in Elixir, lightweight processes act like these baristas, working independently yet collaboratively to achieve your application's goals.

Unlike traditional processes in other languages, Elixir's processes are lightweight and fast to create. They are essentially units of execution that can run concurrently within the same environment. Think of them as mini-programs within your main program, each with its own execution state and memory space.

Benefits of Lightweight Processes:

- **Concurrency:** They allow your application to handle multiple tasks at the same time. Imagine a web server – one process can handle an incoming request while another process handles database access, improving overall responsiveness.
- **Scalability:** You can easily add more processes as your application's workload grows. Need to handle more concurrent users on your web application? Simply spin up more processes to distribute the work.
- **Isolation:** Processes don't share memory directly. This reduces the risk of data corruption that can occur if multiple threads try to modify the same data simultaneously. It also simplifies error handling, as issues within one process won't typically affect others.

How Lightweight Processes Work

Elixir leverages the Erlang Virtual Machine (BEAM) for process management. The BEAM efficiently schedules these lightweight processes, ensuring they all get CPU time to execute their tasks. Processes don't directly share memory, but they can communicate and share data using a technique called message passing.

Analogy: Processes vs Threads

It's important to distinguish processes from threads, which are another common concurrency concept in programming. Threads are units of execution within a single process that share the same memory space. While threads can be faster to create than processes, their shared memory can lead to data races and other concurrency issues. Elixir's lightweight processes, on the other hand, provide a more robust and scalable approach to concurrency.

Example: Using a Process for Background Tasks

Imagine you have a web application that needs to send a confirmation email after a user signs up. Using a lightweight process, you can handle this email sending in the background without blocking the main thread that's responsible for handling user requests. This keeps your web application responsive for other users.

Elixir

```
def send_confirmation_email(user_email) do
  # Simulate sending an email
  IO.puts "Sending confirmation email to #{user_email}"
  Process.sleep(1000)  # Simulate email sending time
end
# Spawn a new process to handle the email sending
Process.spawn(fn ->
send_confirmation_email("user@example.com") end)

IO.puts "User signup complete!"  # This won't be blocked by the
email sending process
```

In this example, the send_confirmation_email function is run in a separate process spawned using Process.spawn. This allows the main process to continue handling user requests while the email is being sent in the background.

Here are some additional examples and code snippets to further illustrate lightweight processes in Elixir:

Example: Handling Multiple Web Requests Concurrently

Imagine a simple web server that responds to two different URLs:

```elixir
Elixir
defmodule MyServer do
  def start do
    spawn(fn -> handle_request("/users") end)
    spawn(fn -> handle_request("/products") end)
    IO.puts "Server started!"
  end
  def handle_request(url) do
    # Simulate processing a request
    IO.puts "Handling request for #{url}"
    Process.sleep(500)  # Simulate processing time
  end
end

MyServer.start()
```

In this example, we spawn two separate processes using Process.spawn. Each process handles a specific URL (/users or /products). This allows the server to handle incoming requests concurrently, improving performance.

Example: Using a GenServer for Maintaining Shared State

While processes are isolated, you can use a special type of process called a GenServer (Generic Server) to manage shared state between processes in a controlled way. Here's a simplified illustration:

```elixir
Elixir
defmodule Counter do
```

```elixir
use GenServer
def start_link(_) do
  GenServer.start_link(__MODULE__, 0, name: :counter)
end
def handle_call(:increment, _from, count) do
  {:reply, count + 1, count + 1}
end

def handle_cast(:increment, count) do
  {:noreply, count + 1}
end
def init(initial_value) do
  {:ok, initial_value}
end
end
# Get the current counter value from a process
counter_pid = Counter.start_link()
{value, _} = GenServer.call(counter_pid, :increment)
IO.puts "Current count: #{value}"
```

This example showcases a simplified GenServer that keeps track of a counter value. Processes can interact with the GenServer using GenServer.call or GenServer.cast to increment the counter. This demonstrates how processes can share state in a controlled manner using GenServers.

These examples provide a glimpse into the power of lightweight processes in Elixir. By understanding their benefits and how to use them effectively, you can build robust and scalable applications that can handle complex workloads efficiently.

Lightweight processes are a fundamental concept in Elixir that empowers you to build highly scalable and responsive applications. By leveraging concurrency effectively, you can create applications that can handle even the most demanding workloads. In the next section, we'll explore how processes communicate with each other using message passing, a key technique for building robust concurrent systems in Elixir.

5.2 Message Passing

Imagine a bustling team of construction workers. While they work on different tasks, they need to communicate effectively to ensure the project progresses smoothly. Similarly, in Elixir's world of lightweight processes, message passing acts as the communication channel that allows processes to collaborate and share information.

What is Message Passing?

Unlike traditional shared memory approaches, Elixir processes don't directly access each other's memory. Instead, they communicate by sending and receiving messages. These messages can contain any data you need to share, like instructions, data values, or even requests for information.

How Does Message Passing Work?

- **Sending Messages:** The send function is used to send a message from one process to another. You specify the recipient process (identified by its Process Identifier or PID) and the message content.

- **Receiving Messages:** The receive or receive1 functions are used by a process to wait for and receive messages. The received message can then be used within the process logic.

Benefits of Message Passing:

- **Decoupling:** Processes don't need to know the internal workings of each other. They simply send and receive messages, promoting modularity and maintainability of your code.
- **Reliability:** Messages are delivered asynchronously, meaning the sender doesn't block waiting for a response. This improves overall application responsiveness.
- **Error Handling:** Since processes are isolated, message passing helps you manage errors more effectively, as issues in one process don't typically affect others.

Examples of Message Passing

- **Worker Processes:** Imagine a process that handles image uploads. It receives a message containing the image data from another process, performs the upload, and sends a confirmation message back.

- **Supervisor Processes:** A supervisor process might send messages to worker processes to check their health or instruct them to restart if they crash.

Code Example: Sending and Receiving Messages

Here's a simple example demonstrating message passing:

Elixir

```
defmodule Sender do
  def send_message(receiver_pid, message) do
    Process.send(receiver_pid, message)
  end
end
defmodule Receiver do
  def handle_message(message) do
    IO.puts "Received message: #{message}"
  end
  def start do
    receive do
      message -> handle_message(message)
    end
  end
end
# Spawn a receiver process
receiver_pid = spawn(fn -> Receiver.start() end)
# Send a message from another process
Sender.send_message(receiver_pid, "Hello from the sender!")
```

In this example, the Sender process uses Process.send to send a message to the Receiver process identified by its PID. The Receiver process waits for a message using receive and then prints the received message.

Here are some additional examples and code snippets to further illustrate message passing in Elixir:

Example: Worker Process with Message Passing

Imagine a process that validates user input:

Elixir

```
defmodule InputValidator do
  def validate(data) do
    # Simulate validation logic
    IO.puts "Validating data: #{data}"
    if valid?(data) do
      {:valid, data}
    else
      {:error, "Invalid data"}
    end
  end
  def start(link_to) ->
    spawn(fn ->
      receive do
        {:validate, data} ->
          response = validate(data)
          send(link_to, response)
        after
          :noreply
        end
      end
    end)
  end
end
# Spawn a validator process
validator_pid = InputValidator.start(self())
# Send data for validation from another process
send(validator_pid, {:validate, "user input"})
receive do
  {:valid, data} ->
    IO.puts "Data is valid: #{data}"
  {:error, message} ->
    IO.puts "Error: #{message}"
```

end

In this example, the InputValidator process receives data for validation through a message. It validates the data and sends a response message back to the sender process (identified by self() in this case). This demonstrates how processes can delegate tasks and share results using message passing.

Example: Supervisor Process with Message Passing

A supervisor process can use message passing to monitor and manage worker processes:

```Elixir
defmodule WorkerSupervisor do
  use Supervisor
  def start_link() do
    Supervisor.start_link(__MODULE__, :ok, [])
  end
  def init() do
    child_spec = [worker: Worker, restart: :transient]
    {:ok, child_spec}
  end
  def restart_worker(worker_pid) do
    GenServer.cast(worker_pid, :restart)
  end
end
defmodule Worker do
  def handle_cast(:restart, _from) do
    IO.puts "Worker restarting..."
    {:noreply, []}
  end
  def init() do
    {:ok, nil}
  end
end
# Start the supervisor process
supervisor_pid = WorkerSupervisor.start_link()
```

```
# Simulate a worker crash
send(supervisor_pid, {:DOWN, :worker, :process, :terminated})
# The supervisor can send a restart message to the worker
WorkerSupervisor.restart_worker(worker_pid)
```

In this example, the WorkerSupervisor process monitors a worker process. If the worker crashes (simulated by sending a DOWN message), the supervisor can send a message to the worker to trigger a restart. This demonstrates how message passing can be used for process supervision and fault tolerance.

These examples showcase the versatility of message passing in Elixir. By leveraging messages for communication and coordination, you can design complex concurrent applications with well-defined interactions between processes.

Message passing is a fundamental concept in building concurrent applications with Elixir. By understanding how processes communicate through messages, you can create well-structured and robust systems that can effectively distribute tasks and share information. In the next section, we'll explore how message passing is used to build even more sophisticated concurrent applications with techniques like supervision trees and GenServers.

5.3 Building Scalable Applications with Processes

Elixir's lightweight processes and message passing are the building blocks for creating highly scalable and responsive applications. By leveraging these features effectively, you can handle increasing workloads and user traffic without compromising performance. Here's how processes empower your applications:

1. Handling Concurrent Requests:

Imagine a web application with high user traffic. With Elixir processes, you can handle multiple user requests simultaneously. A separate process can be spawned for each incoming request. This process can handle tasks like fetching data from a database or rendering a response, freeing up the main process to handle new requests quickly. This improves the overall responsiveness of your application for all users.

Example: Handling Concurrent Web Requests

Elixir
```
defmodule MyApp do
  def handle_request(request) do
    spawn(fn -> process_request(request) end)
  end
  def process_request(request) do
    # Simulate processing a request
    IO.puts "Processing request: #{request}"
    Process.sleep(500)  # Simulate processing time
  end
  def start do
    accept_loop()
  end
  def accept_loop do
    receive do
      request -> handle_request(request)
    end
    accept_loop()
  end
end
```

In this example, the MyApp web server spawns a new process for each incoming request. This allows the server to handle multiple requests concurrently, improving responsiveness.

2. Background Tasks

Processes are ideal for handling long-running background tasks that don't require immediate interaction. Imagine sending confirmation emails or processing large datasets. These tasks can be handled by separate processes, preventing them from blocking the main process responsible for handling user requests. This keeps your application responsive for users.

Example: Sending Confirmation Emails in a Background Process

Elixir

```elixir
def send_confirmation_email(user_email) do
  # Simulate sending an email
  IO.puts "Sending confirmation email to #{user_email}"
  Process.sleep(1000)  # Simulate email sending time
end
defmodule MyHandler do
  def handle_signup(user_data) do
    # ... process signup logic ...
    spawn(fn -> send_confirmation_email(user_data.email) end)
  end
end
```

In this example, the send_confirmation_email function is run in a separate process spawned by the MyHandler module. This ensures that user signup processing isn't blocked by email sending.

3. Fault Tolerance:

Processes provide inherent fault tolerance. If a process crashes, it can be restarted without affecting other processes in your application. This improves the overall reliability of your system. Imagine a process handling database access crashing. By restarting the process, your application can recover without needing a complete system reboot.

Example: Supervisor Processes for Fault Tolerance

Supervisor processes can be used to manage and monitor worker processes. They can automatically restart crashed worker processes, ensuring your application remains functional.

Here are some additional examples and code snippets to further illustrate how processes contribute to building scalable applications in Elixir:

Example: Scaling a Chat Application with Processes

Imagine a chat application where multiple users can chat simultaneously. You can use processes to handle each user's connection and message processing:

```elixir
defmodule ChatHandler do
  def handle_connect(socket) do
    spawn(fn -> handle_user(socket) end)
  end
  def handle_user(socket) do
    receive do
      message -> handle_message(socket, message)
    after
      :noreply
    end
  end
  def handle_message(socket, message) do
    # Process and broadcast the message to other users
    IO.puts "User sent message: #{message}"
  end
end
```

In this example, the ChatHandler spawns a separate process for each user connection. This allows the server to handle messages from multiple users concurrently, improving scalability as more users join the chat.

Example: Processing Large Datasets with Worker Processes

Imagine processing a large dataset stored in a file. You can use worker processes to distribute the processing load:

```elixir
defmodule DataProcessor do
  def process_file(filename) do
    chunk_size = 1000
    chunks = File.stream!(filename, chunk_size: chunk_size)
    Enum.each(chunks, &spawn(fn -> process_chunk(&1) end))
```

```
  end
  def process_chunk(chunk) do
    # Process each chunk of data
    IO.puts "Processing data chunk..."
  end
end
```

In this example, the DataProcessor splits the file into chunks and spawns a separate process for each chunk. This allows for parallel processing of the data, improving overall processing speed.

These examples showcase how processes can be used to distribute tasks, handle background jobs, and improve the overall scalability of your Elixir applications. By leveraging concurrency effectively, you can create systems that can grow and adapt to increasing demands.

Lightweight processes and message passing are fundamental concepts for building scalable and robust applications in Elixir. By understanding how to leverage these features effectively, you can create applications that can handle demanding workloads and provide a seamless user experience. In the next chapters, we'll explore even more advanced techniques like supervision trees and GenServers, which further empower you to build complex and fault-tolerant concurrent systems in Elixir.

Chapter 6: Building Powerful Backends with Elixir

Welcome back, Elixir enthusiasts! We've explored the core concepts of this fantastic language – pattern matching, processes, and message passing. Now, it's time to dive into the world of frameworks! Think of frameworks as pre-built toolkits that can supercharge your backend development in Elixir. In this chapter, we'll be focusing on two popular choices: Phoenix and Ecto.

6.1 Phoenix

In the realm of Elixir backend development, Phoenix emerges as a shining star. This full-stack web framework simplifies and streamlines the process of building modern web applications and APIs. Imagine you're crafting a social media platform, an e-commerce store, or any application requiring a powerful backend – Phoenix swoops in as your trusty companion, offering a structured and efficient approach.

What is Phoenix?

Phoenix is a web framework built specifically for Elixir. It provides a collection of pre-written code libraries and conventions that expedite development. Think of it as a well-equipped toolbox that saves you time and effort by offering pre-built components for common web development tasks.

Benefits of Using Phoenix:

- **Rapid Development:** Phoenix offers a structured approach with conventions for organizing your code. This reduces the amount of boilerplate code you need to write, allowing you to focus on the core functionality of your application and get things done faster.
- **Powerful Routing:** Routing refers to how URLs map to specific functions in your application. Phoenix provides a robust routing system that makes it easy to define these mappings. Imagine a URL like /users/123 being routed to the function that handles user details for ID 123. This clear routing structure simplifies development and maintenance.

- **Channels for Real-time Communication:** Channels are a unique feature in Phoenix that enable real-time communication between your server and clients. This is perfect for building applications that require live updates, such as chat applications, stock tickers, or collaborative editing tools. Imagine users seeing messages appear instantly in a chat window without needing to refresh the page.

- **Built-in Authentication and Authorization:** Phoenix offers built-in features for user authentication (verifying user identity) and authorization (controlling access to specific resources). This saves you time and effort in implementing these essential security aspects of your application. Authentication ensures only valid users can access your application, while authorization controls what actions they can perform within the application.

Getting Started with Phoenix:

Phoenix provides a fantastic foundation for building web applications of all shapes and sizes. Its focus on developer productivity and built-in features make it a popular choice for Elixir development. Here's a glimpse of how Phoenix structures your code:

- **Controllers:** These handle incoming requests from users (via web browsers or APIs) and interact with other parts of your application to handle the request logic.
- **Views:** Views are responsible for generating the HTML responses that users see in their web browsers. They use templates to define the structure and content of the response.
- **Models (optional):** Models represent the data structures of your application, often corresponding to database tables. They can encapsulate data validation and business logic related to your data.

Code Example: A Simple Phoenix Controller

Elixir

```elixir
defmodule MyApp.UserController do
  use Phoenix.Controller
  def index(conn, _params) do
```

```elixir
    users = Repo.all(User)  # Assuming Repo is configured for database access
    render(conn, "index.html", users: users)
  end
end
```

This example showcases a basic Phoenix controller function named index. It retrieves all users from the database (assuming a Repo module is configured for database access) and renders a template named "index.html" with the list of users passed as data.

Here are some additional examples and code snippets to further illustrate Phoenix's functionalities:

Example: Creating a User Registration API

Imagine building an API endpoint for user registration:

```elixir
defmodule MyApp.UserController do
  use Phoenix.Controller
  def create(conn, %{"user" => user_params}) do
    # Validate and create the user
    changeset = User.changeset(%User{}, user_params)
    case Repo.insert(changeset) do
      {:ok, user} ->
        conn
        |> put_status(:created)
        |> render("show.json", user: user)
      {:error, changeset} ->
        conn
        |> put_status(:unprocessable_entity)
        |> render("errors.json", changeset: changeset)
    end
  end
end
```

This example demonstrates an API endpoint (create) that accepts user data in the request body. It uses Ecto (covered in the next chapter) to perform data validation and create a new user record in the database. The response includes either the created user details or any validation errors encountered.

Example: Using Phoenix Channels for Live Chat

Imagine building a simple live chat application:

Elixir
```elixir
defmodule MyAppWeb.ChatChannel do
  use Phoenix.Channel
  def join("chat:lobby", message, socket) do
    {:ok, socket}
  end
  def handle_in("new_message", message, socket) do
    broadcast!(socket, "new_message", %{user: message.user, body: message.body})
    {:noreply, socket}
  end
end
```

This example showcases a Phoenix Channel (ChatChannel) for handling real-time chat messages. Clients can join the "chat:lobby" topic and broadcast new messages to all connected clients. This demonstrates how channels enable building interactive and real-time web applications.

These examples provide a glimpse into the versatility of Phoenix. By leveraging its features, you can build robust APIs, interactive web applications, and real-time communication features for your Elixir projects.

Phoenix streamlines backend development in Elixir by providing a structured and efficient approach. Its features like rapid development, powerful routing, real-time communication channels, and built-in security features make it a valuable asset for building modern web applications. In the next section, we'll explore Ecto, a powerful database interaction library that integrates seamlessly with Phoenix for a complete backend development solution.

6.2 Ecto

Ecto is a powerful Elixir library that provides a functional approach to interacting with relational databases in Phoenix applications. It offers a clean and concise way to perform CRUD (Create, Read, Update, Delete) operations and schema definitions, making it a popular choice for developers of all levels.

Key Concepts:

- **Functional Programming:** Ecto adheres to functional programming principles, where functions are treated as pure values and avoid side effects. This leads to predictable and maintainable code.
- **Schemas:** Schemas define the structure of your data in the database, similar to database tables. They map Elixir structs to database tables and specify data types and constraints.
- **Ecto Queries:** Ecto provides a builder pattern for constructing database queries. You chain methods together to define the desired operation and filter criteria.

- **Changesets:** Changesets are used to validate and prepare data for insertion or update operations. They encapsulate data manipulation logic and ensure data integrity.

Benefits of Ecto:

- **Improved Code Readability:** Ecto's functional style leads to clear and concise code that is easy to understand and reason about.
- **Reduced Boilerplate:** Ecto eliminates the need for writing raw SQL queries, reducing boilerplate code and improving maintainability.
- **Strong Data Validation:** Ecto's changeset functionality enforces data validation rules, preventing invalid data from entering the database.

- **Database Agnostic:** Ecto works with various relational databases like PostgreSQL, MySQL, and SQLite, with minimal code changes.

Example: CRUD Operations with Ecto

Here's a basic example demonstrating CRUD operations with Ecto:

1. Define a Schema:

Elixir

```elixir
defmodule MyApp.User do
  use Ecto.Schema
  schema do
    field :name, :string
    field :email, :string
  end
end
```

This code defines a schema named MyApp.User with two fields: name (string) and email (string).

2. Create a User:

Elixir

```elixir
user_params = %{ name: "Alice", email: "alice@example.com" }
%MyApp.User{} |> Ecto.Changeset.cast(user_params, [:name, :email]) |> Ecto.Repo.insert!
```

This code creates a new user with the provided name and email. The cast function maps the params to the schema, and insert! persists the data to the database.

3. Read a User:

Elixir

```elixir
user_id = 1
Ecto.Repo.get(MyApp.User, user_id)
```

This code retrieves the user with the specified ID from the database using Ecto.Repo.get.

4. Update a User:

Elixir

```elixir
user = Ecto.Repo.get(MyApp.User, user_id)
updated_user_params = %{ user | name: "Bob" }
```

Ecto.Changeset.cast(user, updated_user_params, [:name]) |>
Ecto.Repo.update!

This code retrieves the user, updates the name, and persists the changes using update!.

5. Delete a User:

Elixir

Ecto.Repo.delete!(Ecto.Repo.get(MyApp.User, user_id))

This code deletes the user with the specified ID from the database.

Additional Features:

Ecto offers several advanced features like:
- **Associations:** Define relationships between models (e.g., one-to-many, many-to-many).
- **Macros:** Simplify schema and query definition using macros.
- **Transactions:** Manage database operations as a single unit of work.

Learning Resources:

The Ecto documentation provides comprehensive guides and tutorials to get you started: https://hex.pm/packages/ecto.
Here are some additional examples showcasing Ecto's functionality with code snippets:

1. Ecto Queries with Filtering:

Elixir

\# Find users with email "alice@example.com"
Ecto.Repo.get_by(MyApp.User, email: "alice@example.com")
\# Find users with name starting with "A" (case insensitive)
from u in MyApp.User, order: :asc, where: like(u.name, "^A%")

These examples demonstrate how to construct queries using Ecto. The first example retrieves a user by a specific email address using get_by.

The second example uses a query builder to find users whose name starts with the letter "A" (case-insensitive) with like and pattern matching.

2. Ecto Changesets with Validation:

Elixir

```elixir
user_params = %{ name: "", email: "invalid_email" }
changeset = Ecto.Changeset.cast(%MyApp.User{}, user_params, [:name, :email])
# Check for validation errors
if changeset.valid? do
  Ecto.Repo.insert!(changeset)
else
  # Handle validation errors (e.g., display error messages)
end
```

This example showcases data validation with changesets. The cast function attempts to map the params to the schema. If any fields are missing or invalid (e.g., invalid email format), the changeset will be marked as invalid. The code checks the validity before inserting the data, ensuring data integrity.

3. Ecto Associations (One-to-Many):

Elixir

```elixir
defmodule MyApp.Post do
  use Ecto.Schema
  schema do
    field :title, :string
    belongs_to :user, MyApp.User
  end
end
defmodule MyApp.User do
  use Ecto.Schema
  schema do
    field :name, :string
    has_many :posts, MyApp.Post
  end
end
```

This example demonstrates a one-to-many association between User and Post models. The belongs_to macro in Post defines a foreign key relationship with the User table. The has_many macro in User defines that a user can have many posts. Ecto provides functionalities to manage these relationships efficiently.

These are just a few examples of Ecto's capabilities. As you delve deeper, you'll discover its rich features for building robust and maintainable database interactions in your Phoenix applications.

In conclusion, Ecto is a powerful and versatile tool for database interaction in Phoenix applications. Its functional approach and clean syntax make it a valuable asset for developers of all experience levels. By leveraging Ecto's features, you can build robust and maintainable database interactions for your Phoenix applications.

6.3 Choosing the Right Framework for Your Backend Needs

Choosing the right backend framework for your project is crucial for its success. A backend framework provides a foundation for building the server-side logic of your application, handling tasks like data storage, user authentication, and business logic. With numerous options available, selecting the most suitable one can be overwhelming. This guide will equip you with the knowledge to make an informed decision.

Key Factors to Consider:

- **Project Requirements:** Identify your project's core functionalities. Are you building a simple web application or a complex real-time system? Understanding your needs will guide your framework selection.
- **Programming Language:** Consider your team's expertise and preferred language. Popular choices include Python (Django), Ruby (Ruby on Rails), JavaScript (Express.js, NestJS), and Java (Spring).
- **Performance:** Evaluate the framework's ability to handle high traffic and complex operations efficiently. Consider factors like scalability and resource utilization.
- **Security:** Choose a framework with built-in security features to protect your application from vulnerabilities like SQL injection and cross-site scripting (XSS).

- **Community and Support:** A large and active community provides valuable resources, tutorials, and assistance when needed. Consider the framework's popularity and available support channels.
- **Ease of Use:** Evaluate the framework's learning curve and development speed. For beginners, a framework with clear documentation and a gentle learning curve is ideal.

  Example Frameworks and their Strengths:

- **Django (Python):** Known for its rapid development features, extensive libraries, and strong community support. Ideal for quickly building database-driven web applications.

  Python

  ```python
  # Example Django view function
  def create_user(request):
    if request.method == 'POST':
      # Process user creation data
      return redirect('user_list')
    else:
      # Render user creation form
      return render(request, 'create_user.html')
  ```

- **Ruby on Rails (Ruby):** Offers a convention-over-configuration approach, streamlining development. Popular for its developer productivity and large ecosystem of gems (libraries).

  Ruby

  ```ruby
  # Example Rails controller action
  class UsersController < ApplicationController
    def create
      @user = User.new(user_params)
      if @user.save
        redirect_to users_path, notice: "User created successfully!"
      else
        render :new
      end
    end
  ```

```ruby
  private
  def user_params
    params.require(:user).permit(:name, :email)
  end
end
```

- **Express.js (JavaScript):** Provides a flexible and lightweight foundation for building web applications and APIs. Well-suited for projects requiring a high degree of customization.

JavaScript
```javascript
// Example Express route handler
const express = require('express');
const app = express();
app.post('/users', (req, res) => {
  # Process user creation data
  res.send('User created!');
});
app.listen(3000, () => console.log('Server listening on port 3000'));
```

Remember, these are just a few examples. Many other excellent backend frameworks exist, each with its strengths and weaknesses.

Here are some additional code examples showcasing different backend frameworks to illustrate the concept of choosing the right framework:

1. Spring Boot (Java):

Java
```java
@RestController
@RequestMapping("/api/v1/products")
public class ProductController {
  @Autowired
  private ProductService productService;
  @PostMapping
  public ResponseEntity<Product> createProduct(@RequestBody Product product) {
    Product savedProduct = productService.createProduct(product);
    return ResponseEntity.ok(savedProduct);
```

}
}

This example demonstrates a Spring Boot controller for managing products. Spring Boot is known for its rapid application development features and focus on microservices architecture.

2. NestJS (JavaScript):

```typescript
import { Controller, Post, Body } from '@nestjs/common';
import { CreateUserDto } from './dto/create-user.dto';
import { UserService } from './user.service';
@Controller('users')
export class UserController {
  constructor(private readonly userService: UserService) {}
  @Post()
  async create(@Body() createUserDto: CreateUserDto) {
    const user = await this.userService.create(createUserDto);
    return user;
  }
}
```

This example showcases a NestJS controller for user creation. NestJS provides a structured approach for building scalable and maintainable Node.js applications with TypeScript.

Remember, these are just snippets to illustrate the coding style of different frameworks. The actual code for functionalities like user creation will vary depending on the specific framework and project requirements.

Making the Final Choice:

There's no single "best" framework. Analyze your project requirements, team skills, and desired features to narrow down your options. Experiment with a few top contenders by building small prototypes. This hands-on approach will give you valuable insights before making your final decision.

Chapter 7: Elixir - The Elixir of High-Performance APIs

Now we delve into the world of building high-performance APIs using Elixir and its champion, the Phoenix framework. Buckle up, because we're about to craft some seriously awesome services!

7.1 Designing RESTful APIs with Phoenix

In this section, we'll explore how Phoenix empowers you to design clean and well-defined RESTful APIs.

Understanding RESTful APIs

REST (REpresentational State Transfer) is an architectural style for web APIs that emphasizes clear and consistent communication between applications. It defines a set of guidelines for how requests are made, data is formatted, and responses are structured. This ensures that APIs are predictable and easy for other applications to understand and interact with.

Here are some key concepts of RESTful APIs:
- **Resources:** Represent data entities in your application, like products, users, or orders. They are accessed using URLs.
- **HTTP Methods:** Define actions performed on resources. Common methods include:
  - **GET:** Retrieves a resource (e.g., get a list of products).
  - **POST:** Creates a new resource (e.g., create a new user).
  - **PUT:** Updates an existing resource (e.g., update a product's price).
  - **DELETE:** Deletes a resource (e.g., delete a user).

- **Representational State Transfer (REST):** Data is exchanged between applications in a format like JSON (JavaScript Object Notation) or XML (Extensible Markup Language). This allows for flexibility and platform independence.

Building RESTful APIs with Phoenix:

Phoenix provides a structured approach to building RESTful APIs. Here's a breakdown of the process:

1. **Define Resources:**
   Identify the data entities your API will manage. For example, in an online store API, resources might be products, orders, and users.
2. **Create Controllers:**
   Phoenix uses controllers to handle incoming API requests. Each controller is responsible for a specific resource or group of related resources. Controllers define functions that correspond to HTTP methods for interacting with the data.
3. **Utilize Phoenix Routing:**
   Phoenix routing maps URLs to controller functions. This tells the API which function to execute based on the incoming request's URL and HTTP method.

Here's an example to illustrate this:

Elixir

```elixir
# products_controller.ex (example controller)
defmodule MyApp.ProductsController do
  use MyApp.Web, :controller
  def index(conn, _params) do
    # Get all products from the database
    products = Repo.all(MyApp.Product)
    json conn, products
  end
  def show(conn, %{"id" => id}) do
    # Get a specific product by ID
    product = Repo.get(MyApp.Product, id)
    json conn, product
  end
end
```

In this example:
- MyApp.ProductsController handles requests related to products.
- The index function handles GET requests to /products, likely returning a list of all products.
- The show function handles GET requests to a specific product URL like /products/:id (where :id is a placeholder for the product ID), likely returning details for that specific product.

4. **Returning Data:**
   Controllers typically use the json function from Phoenix to return data in JSON format. This ensures a consistent and widely understood format for data exchange.

Benefits of Designing RESTful APIs:

- **Clarity and Predictability:** RESTful APIs follow a well-defined structure, making them easy to understand and integrate with other applications.
- **Maintainability:** Clear separation of concerns between resources, controllers, and routing leads to a maintainable codebase.
- **Scalability:** RESTful APIs can be easily scaled by adding more servers to handle increased traffic.

By leveraging Phoenix's structure and tools, you can design robust and user-friendly RESTful APIs for your Elixir applications.

Here are some additional code examples showcasing how Phoenix helps design RESTful APIs:

1. **Creating a new resource (POST request):**

```elixir
defmodule MyApp.UsersController do
  use MyApp.Web, :controller
  def create(conn, %{"user" => user_params}) do
    # Validate and create a new user
    changeset = MyApp.User.changeset(%MyApp.User{}, user_params)

    case Repo.insert(changeset) do
      {:ok, user} ->
        json conn, %{message: "User created successfully!", user: user}
      {:error, changeset} ->
        conn |> put_status(:unprocessable_entity) |> json conn, %{errors: changeset.errors}
    end
  end
end
```

This example demonstrates creating a new user resource using a POST request. It validates the user data and inserts it into the database using Ecto. The response includes a success message and the newly created user details.

2. **Updating a resource (PUT request):**

Elixir
```elixir
defmodule MyApp.ProductsController do
  use MyApp.Web, :controller
  def update(conn, %{"id" => id, "product" => product_params}) do
    # Find the product and update its details
    product = Repo.get(MyApp.Product, id)
    changeset = MyApp.Product.changeset(product, product_params)
    case Repo.update(changeset) do
      {:ok, product} ->
        json conn, %{message: "Product updated successfully!", product: product}
      {:error, changeset} ->
        conn |> put_status(:unprocessable_entity) |> json conn, %{errors: changeset.errors}
    end
  end
end
```

This example showcases updating a product resource with a PUT request. It retrieves the product by ID, updates its details based on provided params, and persists the changes using Ecto. The response includes a success message and the updated product details.

These examples highlight how Phoenix facilitates building well-defined RESTful API endpoints that handle different HTTP methods for interacting with resources.

7.2 Handling Requests Efficiently with Concurrency

Imagine your API is a bustling restaurant. Customers (requests) pour in, and your goal is to serve them all efficiently without long wait times. That's where concurrency comes in – it's like having multiple chefs (processes) working simultaneously to fulfill orders. In this section, we'll explore how Elixir and Phoenix empower you to handle API requests efficiently.

Understanding Concurrency:

Concurrency allows multiple tasks to run seemingly at the same time. This doesn't necessarily mean they execute truly simultaneously on a single core CPU, but rather that the operating system rapidly switches between tasks, creating the illusion of parallelism. It's like having multiple cooks in a kitchen, each working on different dishes at different stages of preparation.
Here's why concurrency is crucial for APIs:
- **High Traffic Handling:** APIs can receive a surge of requests, especially during peak times. Concurrency ensures your API can handle these requests efficiently, preventing bottlenecks and long response times.
- **Improved Scalability:** As your user base grows, you can add more resources (servers) to handle more concurrent requests, just like expanding your restaurant kitchen to accommodate more cooks during busy hours.

- **Better User Experience:** By handling requests efficiently, your API provides a smooth and responsive experience for users, even under heavy load.

Concurrency in Elixir and Phoenix:

Elixir excels at concurrency with its lightweight processes called GenServers. These GenServers can handle incoming API requests independently, improving overall performance.
Phoenix leverages GenServers to build scalable and responsive APIs. Here are some key concepts:
- **Channels:** Act as communication pipelines between processes. Imagine them as order slips passed between chefs in the kitchen. Channels allow GenServers to exchange data and coordinate their work.
- **Supervisory Trees:** Ensure the health and stability of your application. A supervisor process oversees a group of child GenServers, restarting them if they crash. Think of it as the restaurant manager ensuring all chefs are working properly and replacing any who are overwhelmed.

Here's a simplified code example (without Phoenix specifics) to illustrate concurrency:

Elixir

```elixir
defmodule MyApp.Worker do
  def handle_request(data) do
    # Process the data (simulated work)
    Process.sleep(1000)
    data <> " Processed!"
  end
end
# Spawn two worker processes
worker_pid1 = spawn(MyApp.Worker, :handle_request, ["Request 1"])
worker_pid2 = spawn(MyApp.Worker, :handle_request, ["Request 2"])
# Receive results from workers (replace with actual receiving mechanism)
receive do
  {^worker_pid1, result1} ->
    IO.puts "Result 1: #{result1}"
  {^worker_pid2, result2} ->
    IO.puts "Result 2: #{result2}"
end
```

This example shows two worker processes spawned concurrently. Each can handle a request (data processing) independently. While one process works, the other doesn't have to wait – the operating system efficiently switches between them.

Benefits of Concurrency in Phoenix APIs:

- **Improved Performance:** Concurrent request processing reduces wait times and improves responsiveness.
- **Scalability:** The ability to add more resources allows the API to handle higher loads efficiently.
- **Efficient Resource Utilization:** Processes only use resources when actively working, leading to better resource management.

While the previous example showcases the general concept of concurrency with worker processes, here's an illustration using Phoenix channels to demonstrate concurrency in the context of APIs:

Scenario: Imagine a real-time chat application where users can send messages to each other.

1. **Client-side (simplified):**
JavaScript
```
const socket = new Phoenix.Socket("/api/socket");
socket.connect();
const channel = socket.channel("chat:room", { room_id: 123 });
channel.join()
  .receive("ok", (response) => console.log("Joined chat room!"))
  .receive("error", (reason) => console.error("Failed to join:", reason));
channel.push("new_message", { message: "Hello from client!" });
```

This snippet shows a simplified client connecting to a Phoenix channel for a specific chat room. The client can then push messages to the channel.

2. **Server-side (Phoenix controller and GenServer):**

Elixir
```
defmodule MyApp.ChatController do
  use MyApp.Web, :controller

  def join(conn, %{"room_id" => room_id}) do
    {:ok, socket} = Phoenix.Controller.assigns(conn)
    channel = MyApp.Chat.RoomChannel{room_id: room_id}
    Phoenix.Channel.join(socket, channel)
    # ... (handle successful join or error)
  end
end
defmodule MyApp.Chat.RoomChannel do
  use MyApp.Web, :channel
  def join(conn, _params) do
    {:ok, conn}
  end
  def handle_in("new_message", %{"message" => message}, conn) do
    # Broadcast the message to all users in the room
```

```
    MyApp.Chat.Room.broadcast(conn.assigns.room_id,
"new_message", %{message: message})
      {:noreply, conn}
    end
end
```

This code showcases a Phoenix controller handling room join requests and a GenServer (MyApp.Chat.RoomChannel) managing the chat room channel. When a client joins the channel, the GenServer can handle messages concurrently from multiple users in the room, broadcasting them to all connected clients.

This is a simplified example, but it demonstrates how Phoenix channels and GenServers facilitate concurrency in handling real-time communication within an API.

By leveraging Elixir's concurrency features, Phoenix empowers you to build APIs that can handle high traffic efficiently, ensuring a smooth user experience even under load.

7.3 Building Secure and Scalable APIs in Elixir

Just like a well-guarded castle protects its treasures, APIs need robust security to safeguard sensitive data. In this section, we'll explore how Elixir and Phoenix empower you to build secure and scalable APIs.

Security Essentials for APIs

- **Authentication:** Verifies a user's identity before granting access to resources. Imagine a castle guard checking visitor credentials before allowing entry.
- **Authorization:** Determines what actions a user can perform after authentication. Think of it as the guard granting specific access based on the visitor's role (e.g., guest vs. royal family).
- **Data Validation:** Ensures that user-provided data adheres to expected formats and prevents malicious attacks (e.g., SQL injection). It's like the guard inspecting incoming packages for suspicious content.

Security in Phoenix:

Phoenix provides features to implement these security measures:

- **Plug and Socket Authorization:** Intercept and authorize incoming requests before reaching controllers. Think of the guard checking credentials before allowing anyone near the castle gate.
- **Token-based Authentication:** Utilizes tokens (like digital keys) to verify user identity for API access. Imagine the guard recognizing visitors based on pre-issued badges.
- **Input Validation:** Phoenix integrates with libraries like Ecto to validate user input, preventing potential security vulnerabilities. It's like the guard inspecting the contents of packages before allowing them inside.

Here's a simplified code example (without Phoenix specifics) to illustrate authentication:

Elixir

```elixir
defmodule MyApp.Auth do
  def login(username, password) do
    user = Repo.get_by(MyApp.User, username: username)

    if user && Comeonin.check_password(user.password_hash, password) do
      {:ok, user}
    else
      {:error, :invalid_credentials}
    end
  end
end
```

This example shows a basic login function that retrieves a user by username and verifies their password using a library like Comeonin. Only valid credentials grant access.

Benefits of Secure APIs:

- **Protects Sensitive Data:** Prevents unauthorized access to user information and other confidential data.
- **Enhances User Trust:** Users feel confident interacting with your API knowing their data is secure.

- **Reduces Security Risks:** Minimizes vulnerabilities to cyberattacks and data breaches.

Scalability for Growing APIs:

As your user base expands, your API needs to adapt. Elixir's focus on concurrency and fault tolerance makes scaling your API a breeze. Here's how:
- **Horizontal Scaling:** Add more servers (like building additional castle towers) to handle increased traffic. Each server can handle requests concurrently.
- **Fault Tolerance:** If one server encounters an issue, the others can continue processing requests (like having backup guards in case one is incapacitated).

Benefits of Scalable APIs:
- **Handles High Traffic:** API performance remains optimal even under heavy user loads.
- **Improved Availability:** Minimizes downtime and ensures consistent service delivery.
- **Cost-Effective Growth:** Scales horizontally using additional servers, often more cost-effective than vertical scaling (upgrading single servers).

By incorporating security features and leveraging Elixir's scalability strengths, Phoenix empowers you to build robust and secure APIs that can grow seamlessly alongside your application.

Here's an example showcasing Phoenix token-based authentication with simplified code:

1. User Model (simplified):

Elixir

```elixir
defmodule MyApp.User do

  use Ecto.Schema

  schema do
    field :username, :string
    field :password_hash, :string
  end
end
```

This defines a basic User model with username and password hash fields.

2. Authentication Controller (simplified):

```elixir
defmodule MyApp.AuthController do
  use MyApp.Web, :controller

  def login(conn, %{"username" => username, "password" => password}) do
    user = Repo.get_by(MyApp.User, username: username)

    if user && Comeonin.check_password(user.password_hash, password) do
      {:ok, token, _} = Guardian.encode(conn, user)
      json conn, %{token: token}
    else
      conn |> put_status(:unauthorized) |> json conn, %{error: :invalid_credentials}
    end
  end
end
```

This controller handles login requests. It retrieves the user, verifies credentials, and uses the Guardian library (popular for Phoenix authentication) to generate a token upon successful login. The token is then sent back to the client in the response.

3. Client-side Token Usage (simplified):

```javascript
const token = localStorage.getItem('auth_token');

fetch('/api/protected_resource', {
  headers: {
    'Authorization': `Bearer ${token}`
  }
})
```

.then(response => response.json())
.then(data => console.log(data));

This snippet demonstrates how the client can store the received token and include it in the Authorization header of subsequent requests to access protected resources on the API. The server can then verify the token's validity before granting access.

Remember, these are simplified examples for illustration purposes. Real-world implementations would involve additional security best practices and libraries for robust authentication and authorization in Phoenix APIs.

Chapter 8: Concurrency in Action

Hey there, In this chapter, we'll delve into the exciting world of using Elixir's concurrency features to tackle real-world challenges. Buckle up, because we're about to explore how Elixir empowers you to build applications that can handle multiple tasks simultaneously, making them efficient and responsive.

8.1 Handling Asynchronous Requests with Processes

Ever feel stuck waiting for a website to load a large image or process a lengthy form submission? In the world of web applications, these delays can be frustrating for users and hinder the overall experience. Thankfully, Elixir's concurrency features come to the rescue with asynchronous processing.

Understanding Asynchronous Requests:

- **Synchronous Requests:** The traditional approach where the server waits for a task to complete before responding to the user's request. Imagine waiting in line at a store; you can't proceed until the person in front is finished.

- **Asynchronous Requests:** The server doesn't wait for a long-running task to finish before responding to the user. Think of ordering takeout – you can place the order and continue browsing the store while they prepare your food.

Processes and GenServers

Elixir's concurrency shines with its lightweight processes, particularly a type called GenServers (Generic Servers). These GenServers act like independent workers, efficiently handling requests concurrently.
Here's how it works:
1. **User initiates a request:** Imagine a user uploading a large video file.
2. **Server spawns a GenServer:** The server creates a dedicated GenServer to handle the upload process specifically.
3. **GenServer takes over:** The GenServer starts uploading the video file asynchronously, freeing up the main server to handle other requests.

4. **User continues interaction:** While the upload progresses, the user can continue browsing the website or performing other actions without waiting.
5. **GenServer finishes:** Once the upload is complete, the GenServer can notify the user or perform any necessary follow-up actions.

Benefits of Asynchronous Processing with GenServers:

- **Improved User Experience:** Users don't have to wait for lengthy tasks to finish, leading to a smoother and more responsive experience.
- **Increased Server Efficiency:** The main server can handle more requests concurrently, maximizing its utilization.

- **Scalability:** As the workload grows, you can add more processes to handle the increased demand.

Code Example: Simulating Asynchronous File Upload

Here's a simplified code example (without Phoenix specifics) to illustrate asynchronous file upload with a GenServer:

Elixir

```elixir
defmodule MyApp.UploadWorker do
  use GenServer
  def init(file_path) do
    {:ok, file_path}
  end
  def handle_call(:upload, _from, file_path) do
    # Simulate uploading the file (replace with actual upload logic)
    Process.sleep(2000) # Simulate a 2-second upload
    {:noreply, file_path <> " Uploaded!"}
  end
end
# Spawn a GenServer for the upload
upload_pid = spawn(MyApp.UploadWorker, :init, ["/path/to/file.txt"])
# Send an asynchronous upload request (replace with actual user interaction)
GenServer.call(upload_pid, :upload)
```

```
# The user can continue interacting with the application while the
upload happens
# (Later, after the upload finishes)
# Retrieve the upload status (replace with actual status handling)
{:ok, uploaded_file} = GenServer.call(upload_pid, :upload_status)
IO.puts "File uploaded: #{uploaded_file}"
```

This example demonstrates a basic GenServer that simulates uploading a file. The user can initiate the upload without waiting, and the GenServer handles it asynchronously.

By leveraging GenServers and asynchronous processing, Elixir empowers you to build applications that are efficient, responsive, and user-friendly, even when dealing with long-running tasks.

Here's another example showcasing asynchronous processing with GenServers, this time focusing on background tasks:

Scenario: Imagine an e-commerce application that sends post-purchase confirmation emails.

1. **User completes a purchase:** The user finalizes their order on the website.
2. **Server spawns a GenServer:** Instead of blocking the main server to send the email immediately, a GenServer is created to handle this task asynchronously.
3. **GenServer sends email:** The GenServer composes and sends the confirmation email to the user in the background.
4. **Server responds to user:** The main server acknowledges the purchase order to the user without waiting for the email to be sent.
5. **GenServer finishes:** Once the email is sent, the GenServer can potentially log the success or handle any errors that might occur.

Here's a simplified code example (without specific email sending libraries):

Elixir
```
defmodule MyApp.EmailWorker do
  use GenServer
  def init(_args) do
    {:ok, nil}
  end
```

```
  def handle_call({:send_email, user_email, order_details}, _from) do
    # Simulate sending an email (replace with actual email sending logic)
    Process.sleep(1000) # Simulate a 1-second email sending process
    {:noreply, "Email sent to #{user_email}!"}
  end
end
# User completes a purchase (replace with actual purchase logic)
user_email = "user@example.com"
order_details = %{items: ["Product A", "Product B"]}
# Spawn a GenServer for sending the email
email_pid = spawn(MyApp.EmailWorker, :init, [])
# Send an asynchronous email request
GenServer.call(email_pid, {:send_email, user_email, order_details})
# The server can immediately acknowledge the purchase to the user
# without waiting for the email to be sent.
# (Later, for logging or error handling purposes)
{:ok, email_status} = GenServer.call(email_pid, :get_email_status)
IO.puts "Email status: #{email_status}"
```

In this example, the main server doesn't wait for the email to be sent before acknowledging the purchase to the user. This improves the overall responsiveness of the application. The GenServer handles the email asynchronously, freeing up the main server to focus on other tasks.

8.2 Real-Time Data Processing

Imagine being glued to a live sports feed, the score changing with every exciting play. Or picture a stock market dashboard constantly updating prices, allowing you to make informed investment decisions. This is the magic of real-time data processing – information streams in continuously, keeping you updated on the latest happenings. Thankfully, Elixir shines in this domain with its features designed for efficient real-time data processing.

Understanding Real-Time Data Processing:
- **Traditional Data Processing:** Data is typically processed and updated at specific intervals. Think of a news broadcast with periodic updates, not constantly reporting every minor development.

- **Real-Time Data Processing:** Data is processed and delivered as soon as it becomes available. Imagine a live sports scoreboard that instantly reflects every goal or penalty.

Elixir's Tools for Real-Time Processing: Channels and GenServers

Elixir provides two key features that empower real-time applications:
1. **Channels:** Act as communication pipelines between processes. Think of them as dedicated lanes on a highway, allowing real-time data to flow continuously from one process to another.
2. **GenServers:** Lightweight processes that can efficiently handle incoming data and distribute it through channels. Imagine traffic controllers on the highway, directing the data flow and ensuring smooth delivery.

Here's how these components work together:
1. **Data Source:** Generates real-time data, such as sensor readings, stock prices, or chat messages.
2. **GenServer:** Receives the data from the source and processes it (e.g., filtering, formatting).
3. **Channel:** The GenServer broadcasts the processed data through a channel.
4. **Clients:** Connected clients (web browsers, mobile apps) subscribe to the channel to receive real-time updates.

Benefits of Real-Time Data Processing with Elixir:
- **Enhanced User Experience:** Users receive updates instantly, fostering a more engaging and interactive experience.
- **Improved Decision Making:** Real-time data insights enable users to make informed decisions based on the latest information.
- **Increased Efficiency:** Systems can react to changes promptly, optimizing resource allocation and performance.

Code Example: Simulating a Real-Time Stock Ticker

Here's a simplified code example (without external libraries) to illustrate real-time data processing with channels and GenServers:

Elixir

```elixir
defmodule MyApp.StockTicker do
  use GenServer
  def init(_) do
    {:ok, stock_data: %{}}
  end
  def handle_cast({:update_stock, symbol, price}, state) do
    {:noreply, update_stock(state, symbol, price)}
  end
  def handle_info(:timer, state) do
    # Simulate fetching new stock prices (replace with actual data source)
    new_prices = %{AAPL: 150.23, GOOG: 125.78}
    {:noreply, update_stock(state, new_prices), :timer => :timer.send_after(1000, :timer)}
  end
  # ... (functions to update stock data in state)
end
defmodule MyApp.Web do
  # ... (controller logic)
  def render(conn, %{assigns: %{stock_data: data}}) do
    # Display real-time stock prices using data from the channel
  end
end
```

This example showcases a GenServer simulating stock price updates. It receives price updates and broadcasts them through a channel. A web application can then subscribe to this channel and display the real-time stock data to users.

Here's another example showcasing real-time data processing with Elixir, focusing on chat applications:

Scenario: Imagine a chat application where users can send and receive messages in real-time.

1. **User sends a message:** A user types a message in the chat interface.
2. **Client sends message to GenServer:** The client application sends the message to a GenServer handling chat functionality.
3. **GenServer processes message:** The GenServer validates and formats the message.
4. **GenServer broadcasts message:** The GenServer broadcasts the message through a channel dedicated to the specific chat room.

5. **Clients receive updates:** Clients connected to the chat room receive the message update through their subscriptions to the channel.
6. **Clients update UI:** The chat application updates the user interface to display the new message.

Here's a simplified code example (without Phoenix specifics) to illustrate this concept:

Elixir

```elixir
defmodule MyApp.ChatRoom do
  use GenServer
  def init(_) do
    {:ok, messages: []}
  end
  def handle_cast({:new_message, user, message}, state) do
    {:noreply, update_messages(state, user, message)}
  end
  # ... (functions to update messages in state)
end
defmodule MyApp.ChatClient do
  # ... (functions for connecting to the channel and handling UI updates)
  def handle_info({:new_message, user, message}, socket) do
    # Update UI to display the new message (replace with actual UI logic)
    IO.puts "#{user}: #{message}"
  end
end
```

This example demonstrates a GenServer managing messages in a chat room. Clients can send messages to the GenServer, which then broadcasts them through the channel. Clients subscribed to the channel receive real-time updates and can update their UI accordingly.

This is a basic illustration, and real-world implementations would involve additional features like user authentication, authorization, and message persistence. However, it showcases how Elixir's concurrency features facilitate real-time communication in chat applications.

By leveraging channels and GenServers, Elixir empowers you to build applications that thrive in real-time data environments, keeping users informed and engaged with the latest information.

8.3 Building Distributed Systems with Elixir's Concurrency

Imagine a bustling online store during peak season. A single server might struggle to handle the massive influx of orders, leading to slow loading times and frustrated customers. Distributed systems come to the rescue, acting like a team of chefs in different kitchens, efficiently handling the workload together. Thankfully, Elixir's concurrency features excel in building these distributed systems.

Understanding Distributed Systems:
- **Monolithic Systems:** All application logic resides on a single server. Think of a small restaurant with one kitchen handling all orders.
- **Distributed Systems:** Application logic is spread across multiple servers working together. Imagine a large restaurant chain with multiple kitchens handling orders simultaneously.

Benefits of Distributed Systems:

- **Increased Scalability:** As the user base grows, you can add more servers to distribute the workload, ensuring smooth performance.
- **Improved Fault Tolerance:** If one server fails, others can continue processing tasks, minimizing downtime.
- **Enhanced Performance:** By leveraging multiple servers' processing power, tasks are completed faster.

Elixir's Tools for Distributed Systems

Elixir's concurrency features empower you to build distributed systems with ease:
- **Processes:** Lightweight, independent units of execution that can communicate with each other. Think of chefs in different kitchens, each responsible for preparing specific dishes.

- **Distribution:** The ability to spawn processes on different servers within the network. Imagine assigning different chefs to different kitchens in the restaurant chain.

Here's a breakdown of how distributed systems work with Elixir:

1. **Task Breakdown:** A large task (e.g., processing a large order) is divided into smaller subtasks.
2. **Process Distribution:** Subtasks are sent to different servers in the network, where independent processes handle them concurrently.
3. **Communication:** Processes communicate with each other to exchange information and coordinate their efforts. Imagine chefs in different kitchens communicating about ingredients or order status.
4. **Result Aggregation:** After all subtasks are complete, the results are combined to generate the final outcome. Think of chefs presenting the completed dishes for the final meal.

Code Example: Simulating a Distributed Order Processing System

Here's a simplified code example (without external libraries) to illustrate a distributed order processing system:

Elixir

```elixir
defmodule MyApp.OrderProcessor do
  use GenServer
  def init(order_id) do
    {:ok, order_id}
  end
  def handle_call(:process_payment, _from, order_id) do
    # Simulate payment processing (replace with actual logic)
    Process.sleep(1000)
    {:reply, {:payment_processed, order_id}, {:shutdown, :normal}}
  end
  def handle_call(:fulfill_order, _from, order_id) do
    # Simulate order fulfillment (replace with actual logic)
    Process.sleep(1500)
    {:reply, {:order_fulfilled, order_id}, {:shutdown, :normal}}
  end
end
```

```
# Spawn processes on different servers (replace with actual
distribution logic)
payment_process = spawn(MyApp.OrderProcessor, :init, [123])
fulfillment_process = spawn(MyApp.OrderProcessor, :init, [123])
# Send processing requests to the distributed processes
GenServer.call(payment_process, :process_payment)
GenServer.call(fulfillment_process, :fulfill_order)
# ... (Combine processing results later for final order status)
```

This example showcases two GenServers representing processes on different servers. Each GenServer handles a specific subtask (payment processing and order fulfillment) for a single order. By distributing the workload, the overall processing time can be potentially reduced.

Here's another example showcasing a distributed system with Elixir, focusing on data processing:

Scenario: Imagine a social media platform that needs to analyze user data from different regions in real-time.

1. **Data Collection:** User activity data is collected from various regions (e.g., North America, Europe, Asia) and sent to designated servers.
2. **Process Distribution:** Each server spawns a GenServer to handle data analysis for its specific region.
3. **Regional Analysis:** The GenServers process the data relevant to their region, identifying trends or generating insights.
4. **Result Aggregation:** Analyzed data or insights from each region are sent to a central server.
5. **Global Analysis:** The central server combines the regional data to generate a comprehensive picture of user activity across the entire platform.

Here's a simplified code example (without external libraries) to illustrate this concept:

Elixir

```
defmodule MyApp.RegionalAnalyzer do
  use GenServer
  def init(region) do
    {:ok, region: region, data: []}
```

```elixir
  end

  def handle_cast({:new_data, data_point}, state) do
    {:noreply, update_data(state, data_point)}
  end
  # ... (functions to update and analyze data based on region)
end
# Spawn GenServers on different servers (replace with actual distribution logic)
na_analyzer = spawn(MyApp.RegionalAnalyzer, :init, ["North America"])
europe_analyzer = spawn(MyApp.RegionalAnalyzer, :init, ["Europe"])
asia_analyzer = spawn(MyApp.RegionalAnalyzer, :init, ["Asia"])
# Send data to regional analyzers based on origin (replace with actual data flow)
GenServer.cast(na_analyzer, {:new_data, user_activity_from_na})
GenServer.cast(europe_analyzer, {:new_data, user_activity_from_europe})
GenServer.cast(asia_analyzer, {:new_data, user_activity_from_asia})

# ... (Central server logic to collect and combine regional analysis results)
```

This example demonstrates how GenServers can be used for distributed data analysis. Each GenServer focuses on a specific region, improving overall processing efficiency. The central server acts as a coordinator, collecting and combining regional insights for a broader view.

By leveraging Elixir's concurrency features, you can build distributed systems that tackle complex tasks by dividing the workload and processing information efficiently across multiple servers. This approach fosters scalability and fault tolerance, making your applications robust and adaptable in a distributed environment.

Remember, this is a simplified illustration. Real-world distributed systems involve robust communication protocols, error handling, and coordination between processes. But it demonstrates how Elixir's concurrency features lay the foundation for building scalable and efficient distributed applications.

Chapter 9: Testing and Debugging in Elixir

In this chapter, we'll delve into the world of testing and debugging, the unsung heroes that ensure our Elixir applications are reliable and robust. Just like a well-maintained car needs regular checkups, our applications thrive with proper testing and debugging practices.

9.1 Writing Effective Tests with ExUnit

Building robust Elixir applications requires a solid foundation. Testing plays a crucial role in ensuring your code functions as expected and catches errors early on. Here's where ExUnit, Elixir's built-in testing framework, becomes your best friend.

Understanding Unit Testing and ExUnit:
- **Unit Testing:** A testing approach that focuses on verifying the functionality of individual units of code, often functions or modules. Think of it as testing the building blocks of your application before assembling them.

- **ExUnit:** A powerful and user-friendly testing framework built specifically for Elixir. It provides a clear and concise way to write unit tests for your Elixir code.

Benefits of Writing Effective Tests with ExUnit:

- **Early Bug Detection:** ExUnit helps identify issues in your code during the development stage, saving you time and frustration later when fixing bugs in a complex application.
- **Confidence in Refactoring:** With a comprehensive test suite, you can confidently modify your codebase knowing the tests will catch any regressions (unintended side effects) introduced by the changes.

- **Improved Code Maintainability:** The process of writing clear and concise tests often leads to cleaner, more well-structured, and easier-to-understand code.

Getting Started with ExUnit: A Practical Example

Let's write a simple test for a function that calculates the area of a rectangle:

Elixir

```elixir
defmodule MyApp.Geometry do
  def area(length, width) do
    length * width
  end
end
defmodule MyApp.GeometryTest do
  use ExUnit.Case
  # This line tells ExUnit that this module contains our test cases
  test "calculates the area of a rectangle correctly" do
    # This function defines a specific test case
    assert MyApp.Geometry.area(2, 3) == 6
    # We use the `assert` macro to verify that the area function returns the expected value (6) for a rectangle with length 2 and width 3.
  end
end
```

Explanation:
1. We define a module named MyApp.GeometryTest that uses ExUnit.Case. This tells ExUnit that this module contains test cases for the MyApp.Geometry module.
2. Inside the test function, we use the assert macro to verify the functionality of the area function. The assert macro takes two arguments: the expression to be evaluated and the expected result.

This is a basic example, but it demonstrates the core principle of using ExUnit. You can write multiple test functions to cover various scenarios and edge cases for your functions.

ExUnit Assertions: Verifying Your Code's Behavior

ExUnit provides various assertion macros to verify different aspects of your code's behavior:
- assert: Checks if an expression evaluates to true.
- refute: Checks if an expression evaluates to false.
- assert_equal: Verifies that two values are equal.
- assert_throws: Ensures a function throws a specific error.

By using these assertions effectively, you can write comprehensive tests that thoroughly exercise your code.

Here are some additional examples showcasing ExUnit tests for different scenarios:

1. **Testing a Function with Multiple Arguments:**

   ```elixir
   defmodule MyApp.StringFormatter do
     def format_name(title, first_name, last_name) do
       "#{title} #{first_name} #{last_name}"
     end
   end
   defmodule MyApp.StringFormatterTest do
     use ExUnit.Case
     test "formats a name with title, first name, and last name" do
       assert MyApp.StringFormatter.format_name("Mr.", "John", "Doe") == "Mr. John Doe"
     end
   end
   ```

   This example tests the `format_name` function with multiple arguments, ensuring it correctly constructs the formatted name string.

2. **Testing a Function with Pattern Matching:**

   ```elixir
   defmodule MyApp.ListUtils do
     def head(list) do
       case list do
         [] -> nil
         [head | _] -> head
       end
     end
   end

   defmodule MyApp.ListUtilsTest do
     use ExUnit.Case
   ```

```
  test "returns the head of a non-empty list" do
    assert MyApp.ListUtils.head([1, 2, 3]) == 1
  end
  test "returns nil for an empty list" do
    assert MyApp.ListUtils.head([]) == nil
  end
end
```

This example demonstrates testing a function that uses pattern matching. We have separate tests for both empty and non-empty lists to ensure the function behaves correctly in different scenarios.

3. **Testing a Function that Throws an Error:**

```elixir
defmodule MyApp.Math do
  def divide(a, b) do
    if b == 0 do
      raise ArgumentError, "division by zero"
    else
      a / b
    end
  end
end
defmodule MyApp.MathTest do
  use ExUnit.Case
  test "throws an error when dividing by zero" do
    assert_throws(ArgumentError, fn -> MyApp.Math.divide(10, 0)
end)
  end
end
```

This example shows testing a function that throws an error. We use the assert_throws macro to verify that the function raises the expected error (ArgumentError) when dividing by zero.

These are just a few examples, and Ex-Unit offers a rich set of features for comprehensive testing. By incorporating these testing practices into your development workflow, you'll write more reliable and maintainable Elixir applications.

Effective testing is an ongoing process. As your application grows and evolves, so should your test suite. Regularly review and update your tests to ensure they remain relevant and continue to provide valuable feedback on your code's functionality.

By embracing Ex-Unit and writing effective tests, you'll build a strong foundation for your Elixir applications, fostering confidence in your code and leading to a more reliable and maintainable codebase.

9.2 Debugging Concurrent Systems

Elixir's power lies in its ability to handle multiple tasks simultaneously, a concept known as concurrency. While fantastic for building dynamic and responsive applications, concurrency can introduce complexities when debugging issues. Fear not, Elixir warriors! This section equips you with tools and techniques to conquer those bugs and tame the multi-threaded beast.

Understanding the Challenge:

- **Traditional Debugging:** Imagine a single-lane highway. Debugging is straightforward – you follow the traffic flow to identify the cause of a slowdown.
- **Concurrent Debugging:** Think of a complex freeway system with multiple lanes and intersections. Issues in one lane might indirectly affect traffic flow in another, making it trickier to pinpoint the root cause.
Here's why debugging concurrent systems requires extra attention:
- **Multiple Processes:** With multiple processes running concurrently, it's crucial to understand their interactions and potential race conditions (when multiple processes try to access the same resource at the same time).
- **Asynchronous Nature:** Processes might not execute in a strict order, making it challenging to predict the exact sequence of events leading to an error.

Taming the Complexity

Elixir offers various tools to help you debug concurrent systems effectively:

- **IO.inspect:** Your trusty companion for printing variable values at different points in your code. This allows you to track the state of processes and identify potential issues.

    Elixir

    ```
    defmodule MyApp.Worker do
      def work(data) do
        IO.inspect data  # Print the data received by the worker
        # ... process data
      end
    end
    ```

- **Process Information:** The Process.info(pid) function provides details about a running process, such as its current state and mailbox size. This information can be helpful in understanding process behavior.

    Elixir

    ```
    pid = spawn(MyApp.Worker, :work, ["This is some data"])
    IO.inspect Process.info(pid)  # Inspect details about the spawned worker process
    ```
- **Debuggers:** Tools like iex (Elixir's interactive shell) and pdb (a Python debugger that can be used with Elixir) allow you to step through your code line by line. This enables you to examine variable values and process state at each step during execution.

Remember: Debugging is an iterative process. Don't get discouraged if you don't find the culprit immediately. Use these tools strategically, experiment with different scenarios, and leverage online resources or community forums for guidance.

Example: Debugging a Race Condition

Imagine a scenario where two processes are trying to update a shared counter concurrently. Without proper synchronization, this can lead to an incorrect final count. Here's a simplified (and potentially buggy) example:

Elixir

```elixir
defmodule MyApp.Counter do
  use GenServer
  def init(initial_value) do
    {:ok, initial_value}
  end
  def handle_call(:increment, _from, count) do
    {:noreply, count + 1}
  end
end
# Spawn two processes to increment the counter
process1 = spawn(MyApp.Counter, :init, [0])
process2 = spawn(MyApp.Counter, :init, [0])

# Send increment requests to both processes concurrently
GenServer.cast(process1, :increment)
GenServer.cast(process2, :increment)

# ... (Later, try to retrieve the final count)
```

Potential Issue: Since the processes might update the counter value at almost the same time, the final count might not reflect the sum of two increments (e.g., it could end up as 1 instead of 2).

Debugging Strategies:

- Use IO.inspect within the handle_call function to track the current counter value before and after the update.
- Consider using GenServer callbacks like handle_cast instead of cast if you need to ensure a specific order of message processing.
- Explore techniques like Agent or Supervisor for managing shared state and process lifecycles in a more robust manner.
This is a simplified illustration, but it highlights the importance of careful design and debugging practices when working with concurrency in Elixir. Here's another example showcasing debugging a concurrency issue in Elixir:

Scenario: Imagine a web application where multiple users can update their profile information concurrently.
- **Potential Issue:** If not handled correctly, concurrent updates from different users could lead to data inconsistencies. For example, one user's update might overwrite another user's changes before they are saved.
Debugging Strategies:
1. **Identify Critical Sections:** Pinpoint the section of code where multiple users might access and modify the same user data concurrently. This could be the function responsible for updating profile information in the database.

2. **Leverage Process.info:** Use Process.info on the process handling the update request to understand its state and identify potential bottlenecks or resource limitations affecting data consistency.

   ```
   Elixir
   defmodule MyApp.UserService do
     def update_profile(user_id, updates) do
       # ... (logic to update user profile)
     end
   end
   # Example usage (assuming the update request is spawned as a process)
   update_process_pid = spawn(MyApp.UserService, :update_profile, [user_id, updates])
   # Later, for debugging purposes
   IO.inspect Process.info(update_process_pid)
   ```

3. **Consider Ecto Transactions:** If your application uses Ecto for database interactions, explore using transactions to ensure data consistency. Transactions group multiple database operations into a single unit. If any operation within the transaction fails, the entire transaction is rolled back, preventing inconsistent data updates.

Additional Tips:
- Utilize logging to track user updates and identify potential conflicts.
- Implement unit tests that simulate concurrent access scenarios to proactively catch data consistency issues.

By employing these strategies, you can effectively debug concurrency issues related to data updates in your Elixir web application. Remember, a combination of tools and proactive practices leads to robust and reliable concurrent systems.

Remember: ** By understanding the challenges and using the available tools effectively, you can tackle debugging concurrent systems with confidence. Embrace a persistent and analytical approach, and your Elixir applications will continue to thrive in the world of concurrency.

9.3 Best Practices for Reliable Backend Applications

Just like a well-fortified castle protects its treasures, your backend applications need a strong foundation of best practices to ensure reliability and resilience. Here are some key principles to follow, transforming your code into a dependable fortress:

1. Prioritize Clean and Documented Code:

- **Clarity is King:** Strive for clear, concise, and well-formatted code. Use descriptive variable names, meaningful function names, and proper indentation to improve readability. Think of it as building a castle with well-labeled rooms and corridors – easier to navigate and maintain.
- **Document Your Work:** Comments are your annotations within the code, explaining the purpose of functions, modules, and complex logic. Imagine detailed blueprints for your castle – essential for future modifications and collaboration.

Example:

Elixir
```
defmodule MyApp.UserService do
  # Function to fetch a user by ID
  def get_user(user_id) do
    # ... (logic to retrieve user data from database)
  end
end
```
2. Handle Errors Gracefully:
- **Anticipate the Unexpected:** Errors are inevitable. Implement proper error handling mechanisms to catch potential issues and provide informative error messages. This prevents your application from crashing

and allows for controlled recovery. Think of strategically placed watchtowers in your castle, alerting guards of approaching threats.
- **Return Specific Errors:** Use exception types (like ArgumentError or GenServer.Error) to communicate the nature of the error. This helps identify the root cause more efficiently. Imagine different colored flags raised by the watchtowers, indicating the type of danger.

Example:

Elixir

```elixir
defmodule MyApp.Math do
  def divide(a, b) do
    if b == 0 do
      raise ArgumentError, "division by zero"
    else
      a / b
    end
  end
end
```

3. Embrace Monitoring and Logging:
- **Keep an Eye on Your Castle:** Utilize monitoring tools to track your application's performance metrics (e.g., response times, resource usage) and identify potential bottlenecks or errors before they become critical issues. Imagine strategically placed scouts constantly observing the surrounding lands.
- **Log Your Activity:** Implement logging to record application events and errors. Logs provide valuable historical data for troubleshooting and understanding application behavior. Think of detailed chronicles kept within the castle walls, recording important events.

4. Automate Your Tests:
- **Regular Drills for Your Guards:** Integrate unit tests and integration tests into your development workflow. Automate running these tests frequently to ensure your code continues to function as expected after changes. This acts as a regular drill for your guards, ensuring they remain vigilant.

Example:
Elixir

mix test

5. Leverage Built-in Features:

- **Elixir's Toolbox:** Elixir offers built-in features like supervision trees (Supervisor) and OTP behaviors (GenServer, GenAgent) to manage process lifecycles, handle errors, and ensure application stability. These are like pre-built defensive structures within your castle walls, providing an extra layer of protection.

Here are some additional examples showcasing best practices for reliable backend applications:

1. Input Validation:

- **Protect the Gates:** Implement robust input validation to prevent malicious or unexpected data from entering your application. This can involve checking data types, format, and ensuring values fall within acceptable ranges. Think of vigilant guards at the castle gates, inspecting anyone who wishes to enter.

Example:

```elixir
Elixir
defmodule MyApp.UserService do
  def create_user(name, email) do
    if String.length(name) < 3 do
      raise ArgumentError, "name must be at least 3 characters long"
    end
    # ... (further validation and user creation logic)
  end

end
```

2. Secure Communication:

- **Fortified Communication Channels:** When transmitting sensitive data (e.g., passwords), ensure secure communication protocols like HTTPS are used to encrypt the data in transit. Imagine secret messages delivered through hidden tunnels, protected from prying eyes.

3. Caching Mechanisms:

- **Strategic Stockpiles:** For frequently accessed data, consider using caching mechanisms to store retrieved data for a specific duration. This reduces database load and improves application performance. Think of well-stocked pantries within the castle, providing quick access to commonly used supplies.

Example (using the Cachex library):

```elixir
defmodule MyApp.ProductService do
  @cache_ttl 60_000  # Cache data for 1 minute
  def get_product(product_id) do
    Cachex.get("product-#{product_id}") ||
      # ... (logic to retrieve product data from database) |>
      Cachex.put("product-#{product_id}", @cache_ttl)
  end
end
```

4. Proper Error Reporting:

- **Informative Messages for the King:** In addition to logging errors, consider implementing mechanisms to report critical errors to administrators or development teams. This allows for quicker intervention and resolution of issues. Think of messengers dispatched to the King with urgent news.

By incorporating these additional practices alongside the core principles mentioned earlier, you'll build a comprehensive defense system for your backend applications, ensuring their reliability and security. Remember, a secure and well-maintained application is a fortress that inspires confidence and protects its valuable data.

Chapter 10: Building Fault-Tolerant Systems

We've covered testing and debugging, but what about situations where unexpected errors occur? This chapter delves into the realm of fault tolerance, ensuring your Elixir applications remain resilient even in the face of adversity. Enter OTP (Open Telecom Platform), a collection of robust tools that will transform your code into an unyielding fortress!

10.1 Open Telecom Platform (OTP)

Imagine building a complex system, like an e-commerce platform. You want it to be constantly available to users, even if individual parts encounter errors. Here's where the Open Telecom Platform (OTP) comes in – your secret weapon for building robust and fault-tolerant Elixir applications.

What is OTP?
OTP is a collection of libraries, design principles, and best practices for creating reliable systems in Elixir. Developed by Ericsson for telecom applications that demand high uptime, OTP provides the tools and techniques to build applications that:

- **Self-heal:** Recover from failures without requiring manual intervention.
- **Stay available:** Remain operational even if individual components experience issues.

- **Scale easily:** Adapt to increased load by adding or removing processes as needed.

Core Concepts of OTP:

1. **Supervision Trees:** Processes are organized hierarchically. A parent process oversees its child processes, monitoring their health and behavior. This structure allows for isolating failures and preventing them from cascading throughout the application.
   - Think of a company with departments (parent processes) and teams within those departments (child processes). If a team encounters a

problem (process crash), the department head (parent process) can take action, like re-assigning tasks or escalating the issue.
2. **Error Handling:** OTP enforces a structured approach to error handling, promoting clean and maintainable code. Processes can gracefully handle errors and communicate them appropriately within the supervision tree.
- Imagine each team within the company having a clear protocol for reporting issues to their department head. This ensures a coordinated response to problems.
3. **Hot Swapping:** A fantastic feature that allows you to update your application code while it's running! Imagine upgrading software on individual team member's computers without disrupting the entire company's operations. This is crucial for deploying bug fixes or new features without downtime.

Benefits of Using OTP:

- **Increased System Reliability:** By isolating failures and restarting processes, OTP helps your application remain operational even during errors.
- **Improved Maintainability:** The structured approach to supervision and error handling leads to cleaner and easier-to-understand code.
- **Enhanced Scalability:** The ability to add or remove processes dynamically allows your application to adapt to changing demands.

Getting Started with OTP:

While a deep dive into OTP is beyond the scope of this chapter, here's a glimpse into some of the fundamental building blocks:

- **Supervisors:** The commanders in your application's supervision tree, responsible for monitoring and restarting child processes.
- **GenServers:** Specialized processes that manage state and provide reliable services.
- **Processes:** The building blocks of your application, each with its own execution context and responsibilities.

Code Examples Illustrating OTP Concepts:

Here are some code snippets showcasing basic OTP functionalities in Elixir:

1. Simple Supervisor with One-for-One Restart Strategy:

This example defines a supervisor process (SimpleSup) that monitors a single child process (Worker). If the Worker crashes, the supervisor restarts it using the one-for-one strategy.

Elixir

```elixir
defmodule SimpleSup do
  use Supervisor
  def init(_args) do
    Supervisor.Spec.new([
      worker(MyApp.Worker, [])  # Define the child process spec
    ], strategy: :one_for_one)  # Set the restart strategy
  end
nd
```

2. GenServer Example:

This example defines a simple CounterGenServer that maintains a counter value and allows processes to increment or retrieve it via messages:

Elixir

```elixir
defmodule CounterGenServer do
  use GenServer
  def init(initial_value) do
    {:ok, initial_value}
  end
  def handle_call(:increment, _from, count) do
    {:reply, count + 1, count + 1}
  end
  def handle_call(:get, _from, count) do
    {:reply, count, count}
  en
  # ... other message handling functions
```

End

3. Supervision Tree with GenServer:

Here's an extended example demonstrating a supervision tree with a SimpleSup process overseeing a CounterGenServer:

```elixir
defmodule MyApp do
  def start_application do
    Supervisor.start_link({:local, :simple_sup}, SimpleSup, [])
  end
end
defmodule SimpleSup do
  use Supervisor
  def init(_args) do
    Supervisor.Spec.new([
      worker(CounterGenServer, [0])  # Start the CounterGenServer as a child
    ], strategy: :one_for_one)
  end
end
```

These are simplified examples, but they illustrate the core concepts:
- Supervision tree structure with parent-child relationships.
- Supervisor defining the child processes and restart strategy.
- GenServer managing state (counter value) and responding to messages.

By understanding and utilizing these building blocks, you can leverage OTP's power to create robust and fault-tolerant systems in Elixir. Remember, these are just starting points. Explore the vast capabilities of OTP to truly fortify your applications against failures.

Remember: OTP is a powerful toolkit, but it requires learning and practice. Numerous resources and libraries are available to help you on your journey to building fault-tolerant Elixir systems.

10.2 Supervisors

Imagine a bustling city with dedicated caretakers for each district. These caretakers constantly monitor their assigned areas, ensuring everything runs smoothly. In the realm of Elixir's OTP (Open Telecom Platform), supervisors play a similar role, overseeing and managing the well-being of child processes within your application.

What are Supervisors?

Supervisors are special processes responsible for monitoring and managing their child processes. They act as the watchful guardians, ensuring the smooth operation of their designated sections (child processes) within the larger application (city).

- **Child Processes:** Independent units of execution within your application, each with its own specific task.

- **Supervision Tree:** A hierarchical structure where supervisors oversee their child processes, which can themselves be supervisors with their own child processes. This forms a tree-like structure for organizing and managing processes.

Responsibilities of a Supervisor:

- **Monitoring:** Supervisors constantly check on the health of their child processes. This might involve tracking process uptime, resource usage, or even checking for specific error messages.

- **Restarting:** If a child process crashes or exhibits unexpected behavior, the supervisor can take corrective action. The most common action is restarting the child process, essentially giving it a fresh start.

- **Escalation:** In some cases, a supervisor might not be able to handle a child process failure on its own. It can then escalate the issue to its own parent supervisor within the supervision tree.

Benefits of Using Supervisors:

- **Improved Fault Tolerance:** By restarting failed processes, supervisors prevent errors from cascading throughout your application. This keeps your application running smoothly even if individual components encounter problems.

- **Isolation of Failures:** Supervisors help isolate failures within specific parts of the application. This makes troubleshooting easier and prevents a single issue from taking down the entire system.

- **Simplified Process Management:** Supervision trees provide a clear structure for managing processes, making your application more organized and easier to maintain.

Types of Restart Strategies:

Supervisors can employ different strategies for restarting child processes:
- **One-for-One:** The supervisor restarts only the specific child process that failed. This is the most common approach.
- **One-for-All:** If one child process fails, the supervisor restarts all its child processes. This might be useful in scenarios where child processes are tightly coupled.
- **Restart Strategy:** Offers more fine-grained control. You can define specific rules for restarting child processes, including retry attempts with delays or permanent termination in certain situations.

Code Example:

Here's a simplified Elixir code snippet demonstrating a supervisor process with a one-for-one restart strategy:

```elixir
Elixir
defmodule MyAppSupervisor do
  use Supervisor
  def init(_args) do
    Supervisor.Spec.new([
      worker(MyApp.Worker, []) # Define the child process spec
    ], strategy: :one_for_one) # Set the restart strategy
  end
end
```

In this example, MyAppSupervisor oversees a single child process, MyApp.Worker. If the Worker crashes, the supervisor will restart it using the one-for-one strategy.

Remember: Supervisors are a fundamental concept in building robust and fault-tolerant Elixir applications. By leveraging their monitoring, restarting, and escalation capabilities, you can ensure your application remains operational even when faced with unexpected challenges.

Additional Considerations:

- Supervisors can be configured with timeouts for restarting child processes. This prevents infinite restart loops in case of a persistent issue.
- The supervision tree can become complex in large applications. Proper design and naming conventions are essential for maintaining a clear and manageable structure.

By understanding and effectively utilizing supervisors, you can empower your Elixir applications to handle failures gracefully and emerge stronger.

Here are some additional examples and code snippets to further illustrate the concept of supervisors in Elixir:

1. Supervisor with Restart Strategy:

This example showcases a supervisor using a :restart_strategy with specific retry logic:

Elixir

```
defmodule MyAppSupervisor do
  use Supervisor
  def init(_args) do
    Supervisor.Spec.new([
      worker(MyApp.Worker, [], restart: :transient, max_restarts: 3, max_seconds: 5)
    ])
  end
end
```

Here, the MyApp. Worker child process is configured with a :transient restart strategy. This means the supervisor will attempt to restart the worker if it crashes. However, it also defines max_restarts: 3 and max_seconds: 5. This specifies that the supervisor will only attempt to restart the worker process a maximum of 3 times within a 5-second window. If the restarts exceed this limit, the supervisor will consider the failure permanent and stop restarting the worker.

2. Multi-Level Supervision Tree:

This example demonstrates a supervision tree with two levels:

Elixir
```elixir
defmodule TopLevelSupervisor do
  use Supervisor
  def init(_args) do
    Supervisor.Spec.new([
      supervisor(MyApp.WorkerSupervisor, [])  # Child supervisor
    ])
  end
end
defmodule MyApp.WorkerSupervisor do
  use Supervisor
  def init(_args) do
    Supervisor.Spec.new([
      worker(MyApp.Worker, [])  # Child worker process
    ])
  end
end
```

This example creates a Top Level Supervisor that oversees a single child process, which is another supervisor named My App. Worker Supervisor.

The My App .Worker Supervisor then manages its own child process, MyApp.Worker. This hierarchical structure allows for more granular control over process monitoring and restarts.

3. Supervisor with Specific Exit Signals:
Supervisors can be configured to handle different types of process exits:

Elixir
```elixir
defmodule MyAppSupervisor do
  use Supervisor
  def init(_args) do
    Supervisor.Spec.new([
      worker(MyApp.Worker, [], shutdown: :shutdown)  # Specify exit signal
    ])
  end
end
```

In this example, the MyApp.Worker child process is configured with a shutdown: :shutdown option. This tells the supervisor to consider a process exit with the signal :shutdown as a normal termination and not a crash. The supervisor will not attempt to restart the worker in this case.

These examples highlight the versatility of supervisors and how they can be configured to manage different scenarios within your Elixir application. Remember, a well-designed supervision tree with appropriate restart strategies is crucial for building fault-tolerant and resilient systems.

10.3 GenServers

Imagine a bustling city with specialized buildings like a power plant or a hospital. These buildings maintain their own internal state (e.g., current energy reserves, patient information) and provide essential services to the city's residents. In the world of Elixir's OTP (Open Telecom Platform), GenServers play a similar role, acting as stateful and reliable service providers within your application.

What are GenServers?

GenServers are a powerful construct in OTP that allows you to create processes capable of managing their own internal state and interacting with other processes through messages. Think of them as the specialized buildings in your city, each with a dedicated purpose and its own set of internal data.

- **State Management:** Unlike regular processes, GenServers can store and manage data internally. This makes them ideal for scenarios where processes need to access and modify shared state, such as user information, configuration settings, or in-progress calculations.

- **Concurrent Access Control:** Since multiple processes might need to access the GenServer's state concurrently, GenServers provide a mechanism for controlled access. Processes interact with GenServers by sending messages that specify the desired operation (e.g., get data, update data). This ensures data consistency and prevents conflicts when multiple processes try to access the state simultaneously. Imagine the power plant having a specific protocol for requesting or delivering electricity, or the hospital having a system for managing patient records to avoid conflicts.

Benefits of Using GenServers:

- **Reliable State Management:** GenServers offer a structured approach to managing application state, reducing the risk of data corruption or inconsistencies.
- **Concurrent Access Control:** The message-based communication ensures safe access to the GenServer's state, preventing conflicts between processes.
- **Modular Design:** By encapsulating state and functionality within GenServers, you can create well-defined and reusable components within your application.

How GenServers Work:
GenServers typically follow a well-defined message-handling pattern:
1. **Processes send messages:** Processes communicate with GenServers by sending messages that specify the desired operation (e.g., { :get_data }, { :update_data, new_value }).
2. **GenServer handles messages:** The GenServer receives and processes incoming messages. It updates its internal state based on the message content and defined behavior.
3. **GenServer responds:** The GenServer can respond to messages with replies (e.g., sending the requested data back to the process) or error messages if the operation fails.

Code Example:

Here's a simplified Elixir code snippet demonstrating a basic GenServer that manages a counter value:

Elixir

```
defmodule CounterGenServer do
  use GenServer
  def init(initial_value) do
```

```
    {:ok, initial_value}
  end
  def handle_call(:increment, _from, count) do
    {:reply, count + 1, count + 1}
  end
  def handle_call(:get, _from, count) do
    {:reply, count, count}
  end
  # ... other message handling functions
end
```

In this example, the CounterGenServer maintains a counter value internally. It defines functions to handle two types of messages:

- :increment: This message instructs the GenServer to increase the counter value and sends the updated value back as a reply.
- :get: This message requests the current counter value, which is sent back as a reply.

Remember: GenServers are essential building blocks for creating robust and scalable services in Elixir applications. By leveraging their state management capabilities and message-based communication, you can build reliable and well-structured systems.

Additional Considerations:

- GenServers can be integrated into supervision trees, allowing supervisors to monitor their health and restart them if necessary.
- GenServers can be used for various purposes, including managing caches, handling network connections, or implementing distributed actors.

By understanding and effectively utilizing GenServers, you can empower your Elixir applications to manage state efficiently and provide reliable services within a well-defined communication framework.

Here are some more examples and code snippets to showcase the versatility of GenServers in Elixir:

1. GenServer with Supervisor Integration:

This example demonstrates a ChatRoomGenServer integrated into a supervision tree with a ChatRoomSupervisor:

Elixir
```elixir
defmodule ChatRoomSupervisor do
  use Supervisor
  def init(_args) do
    Supervisor.Spec.new([
      worker(ChatRoomGenServer, [room_name: "Main Chat"]) # Child GenServer
    ])
  end
end

defmodule ChatRoomGenServer do
  use GenServer

  def init(room_name) do
    {:ok, %{messages: [], name: room_name}}
  end
  def handle_call(:get_messages, _from, state) do
    {:reply, state.messages, state}
  end
  def handle_cast({:new_message, message}, state) do
    {:noreply, %{state | messages: [message | state.messages]}}
  end
  # ... other message handling functions
end
```

In this example, the ChatRoomSupervisor oversees a ChatRoomGenServer responsible for managing a chat room's messages. The GenServer defines functions to handle two types of messages:

- :get_messages: This message retrieves the current list of messages from the chat room.
- {:new_message, message}: This message (cast) adds a new message to the chat room's message history.

The supervisor integration ensures that the chat room remains operational even if the GenServer crashes.

2. GenServer with OTP Behaviors:

OTP offers additional behaviors like GenAgent that share some similarities with GenServers. However, GenAgents are specifically designed for read-only access to shared state, while GenServers allow for both read and write operations.

Here's a simplified example of a ConfigGenServer using OTP behaviors:

```elixir
defmodule ConfigGenServer do
  use GenServer
  def init(config_path) do
    {:ok, load_config(config_path)}
  end
  def handle_call(:get_config, _from, config) do
    {:reply, config, config}
  end
  # ... function to load configuration from file
  defdelegate load_config: "__impl__", as: ConfigImpl
end
```

In this example, the ConfigGenServer utilizes an OTP behavior (ConfigImpl) to encapsulate the logic for loading the configuration file. This separation promotes cleaner code organization and potentially allows for hot-swapping the configuration loading logic without restarting the GenServer itself.

3. Distributed GenServers:

GenServers can also be used for distributed applications where processes communicate across different nodes in a cluster. This allows for building highly scalable and fault-tolerant systems.

Remember: These are just a few examples to illustrate the power and flexibility of GenServers. As you delve deeper into Elixir and OTP, you'll discover a vast range of possibilities for building reliable and efficient services using GenServers.

Conclusion

Congratulations! You've reached the end of this exploration into the exciting world of Elixir and its powerful tools for building robust and fault-tolerant applications. Throughout this journey, we've delved into various concepts, from core principles like pattern matching and functional programming to advanced techniques like testing, supervision trees, and OTP.

By now, you've equipped yourself with the knowledge and skills to:
- Design and write clean, maintainable, and efficient Elixir code.
- Utilize pattern matching for elegant and concise data manipulation.
- Leverage functional programming principles to create predictable and side-effect-free code.
- Craft effective unit and property-based tests to ensure code quality and reliability.
- Build fault-tolerant systems using supervision trees and the OTP framework.

Remember, Elixir is a language designed for developer happiness and productivity. As you continue your development journey, keep these core principles in mind:

- **Focus on readability:** Write code that is clear, concise, and easy for you and others to understand.
- **Embrace immutability:** Utilize immutable data structures whenever possible to improve code safety and maintainability.
- **Leverage the power of OTP:** Build robust and fault-tolerant systems by adopting the battle-tested tools and practices of OTP.
- **Experiment and explore:** Elixir offers a vast ecosystem of libraries and frameworks. Don't be afraid to experiment and learn from the community.

The knowledge you've gained is a powerful foundation, but the true magic lies in applying it to solve real-world problems. As you embark on your next project, remember the resilience and efficiency you can achieve with Elixir. Embrace the language's strengths, write code with confidence, and enjoy the process of building remarkable applications.

This book serves as a starting point. The world of Elixir is constantly evolving, with new features, libraries, and best practices emerging all the time. Keep exploring, keep learning, and keep building exceptional software with Elixir!

www.ingramcontent.com/pod-product-compliance
Lightning Source LLC
Chambersburg PA
CBHW082237220526
45479CB00005B/1256